The Modern Nations in
Historical Perspective

ROBIN W. WINKS, *General Editor*

The volumes in this series deal with individual nations or groups of closely related nations, summarizing the chief historical trends and influences that have contributed to each nation's present-day character, problems, and behavior. Recent data are incorporated with established historical background to achieve a fresh synthesis and original interpretation.

The author of this volume, HARRY BERNSTEIN, has specialized in Latin American history for nearly twenty years. He is author of *Modern and Contemporary Latin America, Making an Inter-American Mind, Contemporary Brazil,* and *A History of Latin America.* Dr. Bernstein has coordinated Peace Corps training programs for Latin America at Columbia University and Brooklyn College. A member of the Hispanic Society of America, he is Professor of History at Brooklyn College and Visiting Professor of Brazilian History at the New York University Graduate School.

VENEZUELA
& COLOMBIA

HARRY BERNSTEIN

A SPECTRUM BOOK

Prentice-Hall, Inc.

Englewood Cliffs, New Jersey

PREFACE

The northernmost areas of South America are now receiving some of the attention and interest they commanded long ago, when phrases such as *Spanish Main* and *El Dorado* evoked wide response. As, in past centuries, it brought to fame such figures as Bartolomé de las Casas, Simón Bolívar, and Walter Raleigh, the region today again produces individuals of historic importance: Cheddi Jagan of Guiana, Rómulo Betancourt of Venezuela, Alberto Lleras Camargo of Colombia.

Venezuela and Colombia have not always produced gifted leaders. There are long periods of routine in their history, of apathy, of perfunctory government, interspersed with times of greatness and high purpose. The Independence decade is probably the most illustrious period, and historians must continually return to the national beginnings and the first patriots in explaining present developments.

This region of Latin America tends to be more closely oriented to Caribbean than to South American affairs. The current Panama, Cuba, and Guiana issues and the operations of the Peace Corps all keep the attention of Venezuela-Colombia focused northward. Jungles, great rivers, and high mountains have isolated Venezuela and Colombia from the rest of the continent, while the Caribbean Sea has been a maritime plain, accessible, passable, and also threatening.

Although the main purpose of this book is to trace the rise of nationhood in Venezuela and Colombia and to illuminate the sources of present unrest and revolution, the cultural and intellectual histories of these nations should not be forgotten. The ideas of novelists, historians, and *pensadores*—thinkers—have done as much to shape national values and outlook as the activities of political leaders. A strong humanistic tradition marks the histories of both countries.

Dos palabras: I want to thank my children, Stefanie and Walter, for giving me a leave of absence from my duty to them, and my wife, Florence, for her cheerful cooperation—an invaluable grant-in-aid.

H.B

CONTENTS

VENEZUELA

Colombia

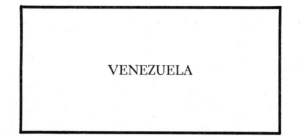

VENEZUELA

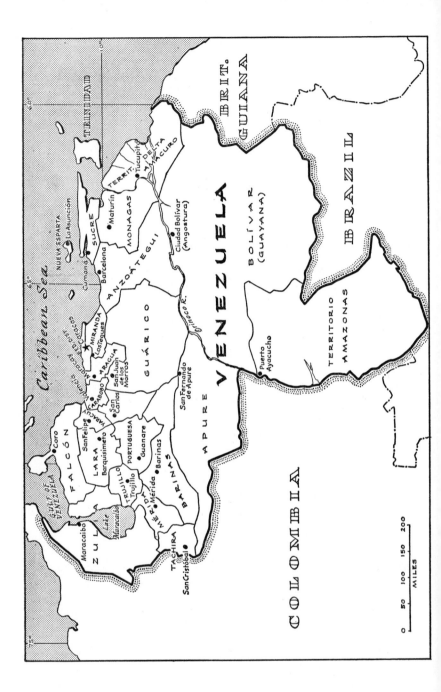

VENEZUELA TODAY

The New Venezuela

The decade of the 1960's marks a new phase in the history of Venezuela. Wracked for centuries by violence, revolution, and dictatorship, the country seems at last to be on the threshold of a new era—an era of new political awareness among the people, new social responsibility among the leaders, and unparalleled economic progress for the nation as a whole.

The new Venezuela may be said to have come into being in 1945,[1] when the political group known as Acción Democrática was ushered into office. The fledgling democracy was to suffer new blows—in 1948, when a military junta seized power, and again in 1950-58, under the dictatorship of Marcos Pérez Jiménez. But the seeds of democracy had taken firm root: in 1958 Acción Democrática and its leader, Rómulo Betancourt, were once more returned to power.

Some of the problems facing the new Venezuela—the extremes of poverty and wealth, the internal military threat—have their origin in the history and traditions of the country. Others—the increasing Communist-inspired agitation, the constant danger posed by Cheddi Jagan's British Guiana and Fidel Castro's Cuba—are manifestations of the international conflicts of the mid-twentieth century. But upon

[1] John E. Fagg, *Latin America: A General History* (New York, 1963), pp. 811-27.

3

its ability to meet and overcome all these challenges may well depend the survival of Venezuelan democracy.

The Rich and the Poor

Few historians have examined in any great depth one of the primary causes of the chronic instability and periodic upheavals which have plagued Venezuela since its birth: the wide and seemingly impassable gulf that separates the rich and the poor. Economic extremes—like political extremism—are still a major obstacle in the path of national progress.

Venezuela is a country of almost unbelievable natural wealth. Vast deposits of iron ore and other valuable minerals lie to the east and the south. To the north, west of Caracas, gush forth the precious streams of petroleum which have helped to make Venezuela one of the most strategic areas in the Western Hemisphere.

Nevertheless, Venezuela is also a country within which is to be found some of the most shocking poverty in all Latin America. Around the gleaming urban centers built and nurtured by oil and mining profits are sprawled the miserable tar-paper and tin-can shacks of the poor. None of the major forces in Venezuela—neither the Church, the corporations, the political parties, nor the military —has exerted its influence to eradicate these shameful conditions and the misery, the immorality, and the apathy they breed. The little progress that had been made in alleviating the lot of the nation's poor has taken place under the aegis of foreign—particularly American—agencies. Perhaps the best known of these groups are the Peace Corps, Acción, and the Creole Foundation.

In the past, the slums of Venezuela have constituted a social stigma—a blot on the conscience of the nation. Today, they may become a subversive force far more dangerous to the country's political stability than any external military threat. Certainly, if Venezuelan democracy is to survive, the gulf between the rich and the poor will have to be gradually narrowed—and finally, perhaps, altogether eliminated. If this is to occur, it will probably not be the result of a sudden transformation on the part of the rich, and hopefully not the result of a bloody revolution of the poor; it can only be the result of a coherent and comprehensive program, carefully planned and conscientiously executed by the government of Venezuela.

Politics and the Military

The dictatorships that followed one upon the other after the exile and death of Simón Bolívar in 1830 left behind no political programs but only a history of oppression and suppression. In this century, the dictatorship of Juan Vicente Gómez, which lasted from 1908 to 1935, was one of the longest and cruelest in Latin American history. His political "doctrine" was one of force, and he gave short shrift to Communist agitators, students' demonstrations, and workers' strikes.

Nor was the military junta of 1948 motivated by any political philosophy or program. The army was enmeshed in its private, nonvoter politics: force, not form, continued to be good enough for Venezuela. And under Pérez Jiménez, Venezuela was more like Batista's Cuba, Trujillo's Dominican Republic, or Pinilla's Colombia. The Venezuela military apparently felt no need to emulate Juan Perón and his high-sounding Argentinian justicialism; it ruled by virtue of its strength and with no lofty ideas about the concept of a nation-state or the *mystique* of public opinion.

To understand the influence of the Venezuelan military on national politics, it is necessary first to understand the role of the military, which may be said to be unique to Latin America. The Venezuelan military—like that of many other Latin American countries—has fought no foreign wars in the modern era. These countries have initiated no attacks, and their own defense against an external military threat is assured by the OAS and the Monroe Doctrine.

Consequently, the military function is confined to police work of various kinds, such as the maintenance of domestic order and security (although the military budgets do not make this distinction[2]). Meanwhile, the untapped energy of the officers finds outlet in the political arena.

During the long colonial period, Spain sought to avoid the rise of this kind of disruptive militarism by supplying her own forces to

[2] Edwin Lieuwen, *Arms and Politics in Latin America*, rev. ed. (New York, 1961), pp. 84-87.

safeguard the security and defense of the colony. In the national period, however, the Venezuelan military has assumed the responsibility for defense against foreign invasion and—with it—considerable autonomy and power. The result is that Venezuelans have learned that their chief enemy is within their own country: the military.

The Present and the Future

How, then, is the present government—and its tenuous democracy —to survive? A nation, like any organism, can survive only if it roots out or renders ineffective those elements within it which impede its vital processes and thus imperil its very existence.

Betancourt's government hopes to begin by "civilianizing" the functions and loyalties of the military. It can usefully assign those officers with any engineering or managerial talent into public works, construction, or administrative agencies. If Acción Democrática can do this, Venezuela will have achieved a revolution within a revolution, and one that could have far-reaching effects. The most powerful subversive force against the government and the new Venezuela may yet be transformed into an instrument for the public and national welfare.

This will take time, but a start has already been made. Before the process is completed, it will have required the retirement of many older officers and the promotion of many junior officers. But when it is completed, the new Venezuela—like Mexico after its own revolution—will have "nationalized" the army, giving a twentieth-century direction to national history.

However successful the government may be in eliminating the threat of the Right, it will nevertheless have to find a way to deal effectively with the even greater danger posed by the Left: the Communist Party, the FALN (Armed Forces for National Liberation), and the Movement for Revolutionary Action, all of which have proclaimed their own violent programs for national "liberation."

Although these recently formed guerrilla-like groups occupy no territorial base (as they do in Cuba and Southeast Asia), and although most of the violence they instigate has been largely confined to Caracas, hit-and-run terrorism has broken out in different sections of the country. These subversive groups can never be incorporated by the government into any socially or economically important government offices and agencies. Such an action would lend an aura of legality to their activities and confront the government with a powerful and firmly entrenched fifth column. Nothing could be worse for the government and for the nation.

Consequently, the government's policy is the negative one of repression. It has attempted to outlaw the Communist Party and the various leftist groups, but the supreme court and the political majority in the congress have opposed these moves. A far more effective weapon is the program of socioeconomic reforms, through which the government hopes to remove the causes for the unrest which finds expression in subversive activity. In implementing its program, however, the government will have to continue to tread a dangerously narrow path between the power-seeking forces of Right and Left.

When it first rose to power in 1945, Acción Democrática had strong socialist views. So did Betancourt himself. To carry out its radical program (on the basis of which it had won office), Acción Democrática was forced to rely on the support of junior military officers as well as on that of the students and the reformers. Government offices were distributed among the young military men and the veteran revolutionaries. The compromise between the two groups made it possible for Acción Democrática to carry out some of its campaign promises. Corporation taxes were introduced (although these tended to deal with the results of poverty, rather than with its causes), and some public lands were divided and distributed among the masses. The division of private estates was ardently debated, but there was little or no expropriation. A combination of earnest intentions and generous promises gave a strong spirit to the new era. But the military coup in 1948 brought all reforms to an end.

When Acción Democrática was returned to office in 1958, the radical socialism of its earlier years had been modified into a left-of-center social and economic program. Betancourt, too, had abandoned his youthful adherence to Marxist Communism, with its emphasis on the urban proletariat, and had developed a concern for the expansion of industry and the security of the small landowners.

In spite of at least one attempt on his life, and in spite of the unceasing terrorist activities of various guerrilla groups, Betancourt had all the time he needed to become the voice of Venezuelan economic and social progress. His work was made more difficult by the opposition of the basic social forces in Venezuela: the Church, the universities, the military, the unions, the large corporations, the peasants, and the upper classes. Betancourt often lost the support of one group while courting that of another: efforts to help the peasants did not endear him to the trade unionists; proposals for public education caused alarm within the Church hierarchy; benefits extended to foreign corporations antagonized the workers. The Venezuelan government—the most powerful institution of all—did not ally itself with any of these groups and tried to stay above the conflicts of interest among them. It has focussed its attention on introducing reforms in agriculture, housing, and education, and on passing laws concerning civil service standards and a social security program.

In addition, the government has tried to free itself from its financial dependence on oil, although keeping up production and revenues. It has also stimulated and supported the industrialization of eastern Venezuela and has aided the resurgence of the ranching and rural areas of the country.

The government's Four-Year Plan for social and economic welfare met with mixed reactions. Because there are many more *campesinos* (peasants) than *obreros* (city workers), the expected benefits were more widely distributed (and the program therefore more popular) among the majority group. The land reform of 1960 was intended to provide an incentive for increased farm production by granting and recognizing ownership of land.

But industrialization was not neglected: grants of public land, credits, and aid to campesinos went hand in hand with the development of hydroelectric power and the encouragement of the petrochemicals, steel, and oil industries. Industrialization not only provides employment (thereby eliminating one of the causes of class struggle), it also produces enormous revenues. The revenues from oil and iron ore continue to be the largest source of government income in Venezuela, and the means through which Acción Democrática hopes to implement its Four-Year Plan and its program for the social and economic progress of the nation.

Whether the era of Acción Democrática will endure is hard to say. Since 1958, many students and intellectuals and the great masses of people have begun to take a part in the national life.

Social demands are being voiced more and more strongly. The new forces urge faster forward movement; others argue that a slower pace makes for more enduring gains. Some groups want to use force to bring about a swift transformation; others want to use force to turn the clock back or to stop its ticking altogether. Both sides are angry; both sides are determined.

The threat of strikes, disputes, and Communist subversion continues. The leading Venezuelan Communist, Gustavo Machado, who spent years in prison or in exile during the Gómez dictatorship, has reappeared on the agitated national scene. The new Venezuela, with its plans for social reform and its liberal-civilian democracy, sees in nearby Cuba and Venezuela and British Guiana—and in distant China and Eastern Europe—the revolutionary power and momentum of twentieth-century Communism.

These are the challenges Venezuela faces in the middle of the twentieth century. These are the challenges it must meet and overcome if the new Venezuela is to survive.

TWO

SETTLEMENT AND EARLIEST YEARS

The Coming of the White Men

Columbus and his men, the first Europeans to see Venezuela, discovered the new country in 1498, on their third voyage to the Western Hemisphere. They found Trinidad, then sailed along the coast to discover a huge amount of fresh water pouring into the sea through four of the seventy mouths of the Orinoco River. Unfamiliar with the enormous amounts of water poured out by the great New World rivers, Columbus called the new land an island, and sailed north through the Caribbean. His total stay in northeastern Venezuela, including landings and short surveys, amounted to two weeks August 1-15, 1498).

Alonso de Ojeda, a later explorer, went from the Orinoco past Trinidad, then west along the coast to Lake Maracaibo. He called the region around the lake *Veneuela*, or "little Venice." Ojeda also followed up the discoveries of others all the way west to Cartagena and Panama. The Spaniards, however, did little before 1520 to establish permanent sites or settlements in eastern Venezuela. They were primarily interested in enslaving the Indians and fishing for pearls. On the heels of the soldiers came the Franciscan and Dominican friars. They reached Cumaná, a site on the eastern mainland south of the island of Margarita, about 1515.

After Columbus, the next most famous name in Venezuelan history is Bartolomé de las Casas, the friend of the Indians.[1] Las Casas arrived sometime between 1518 and 1520, bringing with him both social and spiritual intentions. His well-known experiment was intended to civilize the Indians by keeping away soldiers and *conquistadores*. He also hoped to bring farmers or skilled craft workers from Spain to teach the Indian. The great opposition to his advanced ideas (which included the abolition of Indian slavery) finally forced Las Casas to give up his Utopia. Las Casas' ideas contained the seeds of present-day socioagrarian aims in Venezuela: the free Indian alongside the Spanish-descended *campesino*. Las Casas went on from his Venezuelan experiences to preach social justice for all Indo-America.

Puerto Rico and Santo Domingo organized the further settlement of the mainland. Santo Domingo was the base of government; Puerto Rico was the source of soldiers.[2] Slave raids, missionary work, pearl fishing, and expeditions to *tierra firme* (as the mainland was called) preceded such settlement. Indian resistance prevented exploration inland from the coast. The northeastern region of Venezuela, with its earliest capital at Cúmaná, was separated from the western province. Explorers such as Diego de Ordaz followed the Orinoco up to the point at which it meets the Meta. Great difficulties and disasters led to the comparative neglect of northeastern Venezuela until 1569, when settlers gradually and steadily began to arrive.

The real settlement of Venezuela began in the west. The coastal area between Maracaibo and Santa Marta (Colombia) proved to be the most effective point of penetration. A short time after Coro was founded, two German banking houses were given a concession in these western regions. The German house of Welser sent its agents to take over the lands, to subdue and enslave the Indians, and to start the search for gold. (For a while the German efforts brought together eastern Colombia and western Venezuela.) The Germans promptly moved inland from their base at Coro. They climbed the Andes and reached Bogotá in 1538, just as two Spanish expeditions arrived from the north and south. The Germans, like the Spanish, had

---

[1] Las Casas, who lived 90 years, has already had a far longer life span in historical literature. Controversy about him continues to provide material for innumerable articles, essays, and books.

[2] Bernard Moses, *The Spanish Dependencies in South America: An Introduction to the History of their Civilization*, 2 vols. (New York and London, 1914).

enslaved the Indians by the thousands while exploring widely through the mountain and plains districts.

The Spaniards resumed their own efforts when Charles V, Emperor of Spain, revoked the German grant. The Spaniards then began to move inland toward the east, settling towns, assigning Indian forced labor (*encomiendas*), and establishing missions. The Spaniards entered the valley of Caracas shortly after the middle of the sixteenth century, when they took the site from the militant Indian confederation.

Spanish claims were endangered by not only Indian resistance but also by Lope de Aguirre, who led an uprising of Spanish settlers against the powerful King Philip II in the last half of the sixteenth century. His fanatic and violent rebellion against the Spanish Crown, however, aroused the antagonism of Spanish troops and landowners. He was killed, and with his death the rebellion ended.

After that, French, Dutch, and English pirates and freebooters began to look to Venezuela for their profitable ventures. John Hawkins sold his slaves there and French corsairs and pirates burned and raided Venezuelan seacoast towns. Just before 1600 Walter Raleigh, who led an attack on Cumaná, found his way into the lower course of the Orinoco to look for El Dorado and the legendary city of gold, Manoa. In 1596 Walter Raleigh wrote his *Description of Guiana*, where he had explored. Raleigh's second invasion of the back country of Venezuela took place in 1616. During the seventeenth and eighteenth centuries, Venezuela was exposed to attacks from the sea. By far the most dreaded of British raiders upon Venezuela was the seventeenth-century adventurer, Henry Morgan, who sailed the waters of Lake Maracaibo. During the seventeenth century, the newly acquired British West Indies island of Jamaica became another Caribbean base for assaults on Venezuela. The waters of the Caribbean, better known as the Spanish Main, now became an historic naval route. But Spain still held firmly to the colony.

The Indians

The population of the colony which Spain managed to preserve was Indian, Negro, Spanish, and mixed. Groups of aboriginal Indians occupied all of Venezuela, although they were broken up into many nations, tribes, and confederacies. (Many continue to exist in isolated and remote parts of the country, although conquest, conversion, and intermarriage have reduced their numbers.)

Archaeological knowledge of Indian history and culture is comparatively recent, dating from 1932.[3] Since that time, a prehistoric chronology has been worked out, excavations and zones of research have been surveyed, and artifacts have been examined. Our knowledge is based upon archeological research in the eastern Andes, Lake Maracaibo, Cubagua Island, the Guayana and Guiana areas, the inland regions stretching down to the great plains, and the central part of the country outside Caracas.

The Indians who first populated Venezuela arrived from north, south, east, and west and settled at different times and periods. These were a hunting, gathering, and fishing people. They had none of the great cultural and economic inventions known to later societies. The first groups who knew about agriculture and farming as well as pottery-making came into Venezuela, not from the already advanced civilizations of the Andes, but from the basin of the Orinoco. Presumably, these were the Arawak-speaking peoples, who first moved up along the Caribbean coast and then crossed the islands into the Antilles. Venezuelan Indian culture and ethnology thus shows little contact with that of the Chibcha or of the Incas.

Great divisions of custom, language, and social organization existed in Venezuela, from the Andes all the way to the Orinoco. As elsewhere in the New World, two levels of culture existed at the same time and almost in the same place. The two largest language groups were the Timote in the Andes and the Carib to the east. Dozens of tribes may have once existed within these groups, but most of them have disappeared. The Timote were fine farmers, with permanent fields, which were terraced and irrigated. Many of them still possess work habits and social patterns which lead easily to civilization.

Northwest of Maracaibo, on the Goajiro Peninsula which juts out

[3] J. M. Cruxent and Irving Rouse, *Arquaeología Cronológica de Venezuela.* Joint Publication of the Pan-American Union and the Institute de Investigaciónes Económicas, Facultad de Economía, Universidad de Venezuela: Estudios Monográficos VI (Washington, D.C., 1961); see also *Handbook of the South American Indian,* IV.

into the Caribbean, are the Arawak-speaking Goajiro peoples. They are further distinguished from other Indians in that they are pastoral. Cattle are their chief source of wealth, which in itself shows how well they have learned to use an economic item introduced by the Europeans. They live in a land of little water and no rivers, which is probably the reason why they avoid farming and farm labor. Their herds are the measure of their wealth; they leave farming to poorer relatives. All they willingly "grow" is *chicha*, the Andean corn liquor. The Goajiro do a great deal of trading in milk and meat. Their social system, marital arrangements, and political organization show that, for them, wealth is a source of power and status. They have survived Spanish conquest and colonization, as well as the trials of Venezuelan nationhood.

Far to the south, along the plains leading down to the union of the Meta, Apure, and Orinoco rivers, were the Achagua, one of the most widely dispersed groups in Venezuela. They seem to be the source of the Manoa myth so luring to Walter Raleigh. They once lived in fortified villages surrounded by walls of poles and earth, and their families occupied a circular and communal "big house." (Many of these plains Indians were first discovered when the Jesuits came upon them in the eighteenth century.) Along the same plains were the Guahibo, the most primitive people in Venezuela. They followed a nomadic life in the great savannahs that lead down to the jungle-forests.

The largest group in eastern Venezuela were the Caribs. For centuries Spanish missionaries, soldiers, and historians easily cast the epithet *cannibal* upon them. Only lately has this long-familiar charge been refuted. In 1919, Julio C. Salas, a Venezuelan sociologist at the University of Merida, wrote a bitter denunciation of the myth of the cannibalism of the Venezuelan Caribs and other Indians along the Caribbean coast. The original condemnation is confused by the inaccuracy of historical sources as well as by both historiographic and ethnographic errors.[4]

[4] The Colombianist ethnologist Hermann Trimborn and the Brazilian student Fernando Carneiro have also published their doubts about the myth of Indian cannibalism, and have questioned the reliability of the eyewitness reports, primary documents, and historical source materials. So also has the Argentine Luis Domínguez.

The Negroes

Negroes are also part of the Venezuelan people. Indian slaves were gradually replaced by Negro slaves. The Indian could not be replaced in the pearl fisheries and the earliest *encomiendas,* but the Negro did provide the basic labor on the plantations. Negro slavery had already existed for almost half a century in Spain, following Spanish and Portuguese settlement of West Africa. As early as 1501, Spaniards were permitted to bring their own Negroes to Caribbean America. Negroes were permitted to marry, and by 1517 the Spanish Crown decreed that if Negroes continued to be imported into America, one third of them must be women.

Venezuelan Negroes retained all the tribal, linguistic, physical, and other divisions they had had in Africa. They did not engage in war among themselves as the Indians did. Furthermore, the Negroes brought with them a knowledge of farming, herding, and mining, and made use of these crafts and skills for their owners. The Venezuelan Indians, through contact with the Negroes, adapted to cattle, horses, and ranching techniques. The Indians, especially in the Venezuelan *llanos* (plains), became the famed *llaneros,* horsemen equal to the Argentine *gaucho,* the Mexican *vaquero,* or the Chilean *huaso.* Later on, there were some Negroes on the plains but on the whole the *llaneros* were Indians. Negroes and Indians, especially Carib Indians, sometimes mated but for the most part hated each other.

From the very beginning, the Spanish Crown sought to correct Venezuelan conditions by issuing decrees over both Negro and Indian labor. The Crown used the law to prescribe and regulate social, educational, religious, and other habits. This turned out to be almost impossible. As late as 1789 the Crown was still issuing additional regulations for the education, labor, and treatment of Negro slaves. Spanish royal paternalism lasted throughout the colonial period. Owners were required to support, provide for, and maintain their Negro male and female slaves. Many of them had already provided them with small land plots and holidays, but the law tried to make the practice universal by imposing fines on those who did not. Owners could not get rid of their slaves, even by their generous manumission, without first providing for the slaves' support. Many older slaves were manumitted because that was financially easier for the owner. But this and other laws (such as the one requiring a slave wife to be allowed to go with her husband if he were sold) were not always enforced. Slavery, its financial benefits, and the arrogant psychology of the master had prevailed too long within the social and aristocratic order to be easily changed by laws formulated thousands of miles away.

The Mixed Races

If Negro-Indian (known as *zambo* or *sambo*) race mixtures were rare and contrary to the racial attitudes of both the Indian and the Negro, Negro-white and Indian-white admixtures were very frequent. Much has been stated and written about the mixture of Negro and white in Venezuela, *pardo* being the name the colonials gave to members of that mixed race. But there has been very little scientific study or analysis of the relations among the races. Race was to a great degree identified with caste. The upper classes were almost entirely white. Spanish in origin (creoles or *criollos*), they were in a different and more privileged social order. Indians, Negroes, and *pardos* (*mestizos* or mulattos and, therefore, colored)—who had little to do with one another, if it could be helped—were numerous. The creole families were few (found chiefly around Caracas and other main towns), but had high social position. The *pardos* and other races produced the rank-and-file population of the colony and the nation; the creoles produced the leaders. Race thus meant more than census statistics; it also determined one's position in society and his eligibility for public office.

THREE

VICEROYALTY INTO NATION

The Colonial Capital: Caracas

Caracas became the colonial capital in 1576, almost four hundred years ago. The important political institutions of governor-general and *cabildo* (municipal council) were installed. More towns were founded as periodic wars and expeditions against the inland and plains Indians extended the influence of the Spanish government and the Spanish Church. Finally, overcoming internal bickering as well as foreign invasion, the Spanish government settled down to organize Indians into serfdom, African Negroes into slavery, and white European landowners into an aristocracy. At the end of the sixteenth century, the governor sent Simón Bolívar to Spain to bring back the necessary rules and social orders. Bolívar, the first of that name in Venezuela and an ancestor of the more famous Bolívar, was both a royal treasury officer and a member of the Caracas *cabildo*.

Simón Bolívar came back from Spain with important social and political powers for the governor of Caracas. The Governor distributed lands and services under the forced-labor system of the *encomiendas*. He laid out municipal lands and avenues, provided the earliest town ordinances, and created archives. He enforced the provision that Indians should be compelled to come and live in the towns.

This early Bolívar was also instrumental in establishing the first school in Caracas. Basically a seminary, the school offered scholarships and appointment to applicants who were "descendants of the first conquerors and the sons of those who had served the Crown of Spain with the greatest devotion,"—that is, creoles.

Caracas remained a small town for most of the colonial period. Politically subordinate—first to Santo Domingo, then to Bogotá—Venezuela's trade and produce formed a general part of Caribbean commerce. Fortunately, a rich soil sustained a profitable agriculture and large herds of cattle. Spanish law established a rural aristocracy with the privileges and rights of a nobility upon these former Indian lands:

> The town of Caracas contained about 1500 inhabitants and consisted of two parallel streets running north and south. Two sharply defined classes had already become recognized. An aristocracy had been created by royal order. To encourage the union of the two races, the daughters of the caciques had been ennobled, and Spaniards without rank who married them acquired by this means the privileges of nobility. The nobles having ancient Spanish titles who joined the colony naturally felt themselves superior to the new colonial nobility, but the new nobles enjoyed all the privileges claimed by their distinguished rivals. Between the two classes, however, there existed persistent rivalry and jealousy, which constituted a feature of the society of Venezuela. The antagonism which existed between these classes was a phase of the conflict which marked the relations of the Spaniards to the creoles. . . .[1]

Social and Political Institutions

With the end of the century of epic deeds and European domination of *tierra firme*, the seventeenth century in Venezeula became one of colonial routine and inaction. Priests, civil officials, and Canary Islanders silently immigrated to their offices or labor in Venezuela. It was a quiet interlude between the struggles for conquest and those for independence. No theater, newspaper, university, sermon, or essay aroused attention or discussion. Compared to Lima, Mexico City, Bahia, even Bogotá, Caracas was outside the stream of literary and artistic expression of Spain and Spanish America, both in the Golden Age of the sixteenth century and the Baroque Age of the seventeenth century.

[1] Bernard Moses, *The Spanish Dependencies in South America: An Introduction to the History of Their Civilization*, Vol. I (New York, 1914), 90-91.

Spanish government, society, law, and the Church took hold of the colonial structure and mind. The greatness of Spanish literature and art was no doubt known in Venezuela, but it stirred no creative echo or response. Only in the eighteenth century did the intellectual promise of Venezuela bear fruit.

Production and Commerce

The eighteenth century, which opened and closed with war, brought many changes to Venezuela. The colony had earlier begun to specialize in cacao and tobacco production. Maize, flour, and fruit were undoubtedly important, as was sugar cane, but tobacco and especially cacao were the leading export crops. As early as 1620, Venezuelan merchants had sent cacao to Mexico, and by 1700 Venezuela had displaced the Mexican cacao so important as a crop and currency in Aztec times. Venezuelan cacao not only successfully invaded the birthplace of cacao but also became a world crop. Silver specie flowed into Venezuela in return. Tobacco as well as cacao was greatly desired in Spain, and Venezuela made money through exports to Seville. Cotton and indigo followed tobacco in importance as export crops. After 1800, coffee sales too rose for a short while.

Commerce also bought and paid for Negro slaves. Large numbers of slaves were bought from English and French slavers during the eighteenth century—an age also striking for the profits of large-scale and lasting contraband activity. Unable to buy what they wanted under the Spanish economic system of mercantilism (even though they found their cacao and tobacco market within it), the Venezuelans soon found that the Caribbean was suitable for a free, unpoliced trade with foreigners. Smuggling, independent of the monopolies and restraints imposed by the Spanish Navigation Laws and mercantilism, flourished. This illicit free trade obeyed only the natural laws of supply and demand rather than the artificial laws made in Madrid and administered in Caracas.

Spain could not stop the trade. Venezuela, more than any other Spanish colony, profited from the eighteenth century internationalism in trade. The Spanish Main was now free of buccaneers, but almost wide open to European merchants. In addition, Spain's wars with

France, Holland, and England isolated Venezuela from Seville. Venezuela's trade depended upon illegal access to Caribbean suppliers and buyers. Regular trade was carried on with French, Dutch, and British possessions nearby in the Caribbean (even with Guiana) and British acquisition of Trinidad after 1798 provided a new base of penetration for British contraband trade with Venezuela.

Many places in Venezuela were newly prosperous; some had lost their earlier prosperity. Much of the pearl wealth at the island of Margarita, for instance, had declined. But Cumaná, also in the zone of northeastern Venezuela, became an agricultural, cattle, and tobacco center. About ten miles away were the great salt beds of Araya, "the most abundant and richest in salt to be found in the universe."

The government had already adopted more sensible and pacific methods of dealing with the Indian tribes further inland, replacing military expeditions with missionary movement. Christianity opened up the frontier. Roads and communications were made secure and the Indians were brought down from mountains and woods into communities. The frontier was pushed forward inch by inch, down to the *llanos* and across the Orinoco. Although Dominicans and Franciscans took part in this movement, the Jesuits dominated the internal pacification, settlement, and acculturation of the Indian.

Missionary zeal and pressure led to dramatic social improvements. The Jesuits were also able to get the Crown to free the Indians from forced labor and to put their labor entirely under the direction of the mission fathers. The object was to prepare the Indians for admission to society with full status under Spanish law. In exchange, the Crown perpetuated the European system of private property for both creoles and Spaniards, validating land titles based upon possession and use, even if these titles had not been previously confirmed by viceroys. The Crown, in short, ended the *encomienda* over the use of Indian labor, but made permanent in Venezuela the private ownership of property. This established the landowning aristocracy as a system and as a social class.

The Caracas Company

The most important economic innovation, so far as Venezuela was concerned, was the creation in 1728 of the famed Caracas

Company or *Compañía Guipuzcoana*.[2] The company was owned largely by Basque capitalists, but did its trading almost wholly in Venezuelan products, especially cacao. The company lasted from 1728 to 1785; its rise and decline coincided with that of other basic forces in Venezuela. A joint-stock monopoly, it was designed to check the chronic smuggling and illegal trade, especially that with the Dutch at Curacao.

The Caracas Company sent its first ships to Venezuela in 1730. It took almost two years for its agent at Caracas to get a cargo of cacao to bring back to Spain, so accustomed were the *caraqueños* to do business with the Dutch, who also liked and sold chocolate. Nevertheless, the Caracas Company grew rich, judging from the high returns on cargo, the high dividends paid to stockholders, and the spread of company agencies in Spanish home ports. The Caracas Company also served the Spanish government well. It carried troops during the several late eighteenth century wars, loaded arms and munitions, and even lent its services to support Havana during the British siege and to repulse the British from Venezuela in 1743. The company maintained and supported several regiments in Caracas. It had its own fleet, and provided work for shipyards and innumerable craftsmen, artisans, and mechanics. The company also had license to import Negro slaves. It made every effort to attack and crush its foreign and domestic rivals engaged in smuggling and illegal trade.

The Caracas Company, under its monopoly, controlled both the export and the price of cacao. In addition, it encouraged the wider cultivation of tobacco. As a result of its generally favorable economic position, the company was rich; as a result of its role in war and defense, it also grew strong. It was an important voice of Spanish colonialism. The Caracas Company acquired a powerful position in Venezuela, comparable to that of certain political institutions: the *cabildo*, the later royal *audiencia*, and the university. The Caracas Company also played politics by appointing its friends, agents, and officers to government councils and boards. But the company's activities brought about local resentment, resistance, and even rebellion, and its arrogant officers irritated many officials.

[2] Roland D. Hussey, *The Caracas Company*, 1728-1784 (Cambridge, 1934), pp. 56-60.

The Caracas Company was the first in the history of foreign-owned corporations to extract Venezuelan wealth and sell it abroad. The company set the price of the cacao brought from local planters and the price at which it sold them manufactured goods from Europe. Then the company sold the cacao in the European market at prices much higher than those it paid the planters. Paradoxically, the old mutual need of producer and middleman brought about the equally old mutual rivalry between planter and buyer. The large landowning creole aristocrats, the leading producers, became enemies of the alien company.

Economic complaints merged with political charges against the company. In 1749 Francisco de León, a landowner, led a revolt against the company and sought to drive its agents out of the province. He induced the Caracas *cabildo* to support his complaints. Although de León did not win his fight, the Crown nevertheless reformed the company. Venezuelan merchants and planters were allowed to buy stock in the company and to receive dividends. As time went on, the Caracas Company lost its preferred position. Spanish trade reforms at the end of the eighteenth century permitted freer and direct trade outside the company's monopoly. In 1785 the Royal Philippines Company bought up the shares of the Caracas Company, and the two firms merged.

During the life of the Caracas Company, many changes took place in the colony. After many years the Crown set up a university corporation and body at Caracas, and in 1775 the University of Caracas —now the Central University of Venezuela—came into existence. In 1731 the colony was made into a captaincy-general, and supplementary arrangements in 1786 made Venezuela more and more independent of Bogotá. All the territory later included in the Venezuelan nation came under the jurisdiction of the captain-general. The outlines of modern Venezuela were formed by the end of the eighteenth century. The name *Venezuela* was that of only one of the six provinces which made up the territory: Venezuela, Guiana (Guayana), Cumaná, Caracas, Barinas, and Maracaibo. The governor of Caracas was also captain-general of the whole colony; while the others were governor-intendants.

Military reorganization accompanied political, economic, and educational change:

> The military affairs of Venezuela, like all the other affairs of the colony during the greater part of its history, were neglected by the government in Spain. Viewing the occupation of their possession in America as a conquest, the Spaniards regarded the colonists as soldiers, and were not disposed to make provision for a military class distinct from soldier-colonists. It was expected that the settlers would fight their own battles, and that they were equipped to do this is sufficiently shown by the early history of Venezuela. . . . When a monopoly of the commerce of Venezuela was assigned to the Welser Company or the Guipúzcoa Company, it was expected that the Company in possession would provide adequately for the defense of the country; and it was already recognized that Venezuela was especially vulnerable on three sides: on the northern coast, on the Orinoco, and on the shores of Lake Maracaibo. But it was not until the latter part of the eighteenth century that the Crown found itself under the necessity of constructing fortifications and providing otherwise directly for defense. . . .[3]

The almost continuous wars and revolutions in the Atlantic and the Caribbean from 1776 to 1823 brought more soldiers to Venezuela.

New offices, such as the intendancy, were created. José de Ávalos was the first intendant of Venezuela. The intendant's jurisdiction over land and sea (agriculture, commerce, and navigational waters) made him in some way more important to Venezuelan development than the captain-general was. José de Ávalos undertook as his most immediate task the repopulation and promotion of the island of Trinidad. He extended the privileges of settlers and allowed foreigners to enter and settle, provided they professed the Roman Catholic religion. He distributed land to white settlers, adding an extra portion if they brought slaves with them. His efforts failed because, with the advent of the Peace of Bâle between France and Spain, the British once again turned upon Spain, invading and then annexing Trinidad (1798-1802). The settlers, landowners, proprietors, and slaves returned to Venezuela; Trinidad remained English.

In that same eastern area of Venezuela, Cumaná, the oldest settlement, included territory all the way down the coast past the Orinoco and the Guianas. Spain had created a separate subprovince, Guayana,

[3] Moses, *op. cit.*, Vol. II, 364-65.

in 1762; another royal decree of 1768 gave Guayana the limits of the
Atlantic on the east; the upper Orinoco, Casequiare, and Rionegro
on the west;[4] the lower Orinoco on the north; and the Amazon River
on the south. Because many Catalan merchants found good profits on
the Orinoco in their trade with Barinas, Angostura became the prin-
cipal city of Guayana. One basic weakness in all these arrangements
was the nonsense the Dutch, English, and French soon made of Spanish territorial claims.

War against Spain brought foreign military dangers; colonial revolu-
tions also threatened Spanish Venezuela. The repercussions of the
American Revolution, the revolt of the Andean *comuneros* and the
Tupac *Amaru*, the French Revolution, and the revolt of the blacks in
Haiti were felt throughout Venezuela. Although these revolutions did
not spread by imitation, they did stir up ideas. The American and
French Revolutions, in particular, opened up a Pandora's box of ideas.
Venezuela was the birthplace of the patriot Francisco de Miranda
(1750-1816) and the revolutionary Liberator Simón Bolívar (1783-
1830). Miranda combined in himself the principles of the American,
French, and Latin American Revolutions. A single generation of
young Venezuelans lived through three continental revolutions and
political wars. The American Declaration of Independence and the
French Declaration of the Rights of Man became well known in
Venezuela.

All these points added up to the beginnings of Venezuelan Liberalism. Liberalism at first was not tied to nationalism—i.e., to creole patriotism—but by 1800 had made that connection. Economic forces
slowly came together with the new ideas and political changes of the
day. The most powerful economic groups at the end of the colonial
era were composed of planters and merchants. The merchant guild or
consulado, consisting of wholesale importers and exporters, had replaced the Caracas Company. Like the merchants of Cartagena in
Colombia, the Caracas merchants were economic partners of the merchants of Seville. The two vested interests thrived on the transatlantic
trade monopoly they enjoyed. But their monopoly weakened when the

---

[4] Francisco Xavier Yanes, *Compendio de la Historia de Venezuela desde su
Descubrimiento y Conquista hasta que se Declaró Estado Independiente*, 1840
(Caracas, 1944), pp. 90-94.

many wars and the breakdown of Spanish shipping forced Spain to open its colonial ports to foreign shipping. This competition from foreigners, of course, did not please the merchants.

On the other hand, the planters whose lands and estates actually produced the goods to be exported wanted to be free to sell their cacao and tobacco to anyone who could come and take the products away. Thus economic interests clashed: feudal and slave-owning planters wanted greater freedom of trade for themselves, while the merchants favored their own restricted privilege and monopoly. We have already seen the mutual tie which made the merchant dependent upon the planter's commodity while the planter, in turn, needed the merchant to sell his crops. Nevertheless, there was rivalry, dislike, and competitive lobbying between them. Moreover, the merchants, with Spanish connections, were very often the creditors who lent money or advanced credit to the planters. The planters, who had destroyed the Caracas Company, now found out that the *consulado* stood in the way of their free supply-and-demand trade.

With the British now in Trinidad, the problem grew acute. Merchants protested the decree of 1797, which opened Venezuelan ports to foreign ships (the United States was the chief beneficiary of the decree). The planters, in turn, denounced the merchants in 1797 for interfering with their free export of cacao and tobacco. Coincidentally, a great political event took place in the premature conspiracy of José España and Manuel Gual, forerunners of the movement for independence. From 1797 to 1799, the España-Gual plot provoked drastic counteraction. These two pioneer patriots were caught and executed, but others soon rose to take their place. The year 1797, therefore, seems to mark the end of the colonial mind and suggests the beginnings of independence. During these three years, Francisco de Miranda was in England while young Simón Bolívar had gone to Spain to study and get married.

The Later Colony: Venezuela in 1800

In 1800 Venezuela was still firmly controlled by Spanish absolutism, with all the colonial apparatus of Inquisition, *cabildo*, *consulado*, intendant, and captain-general in control of the situation. Foreign visitors, such as the Frenchman François Depons and the famed

Prussian scientist Alexander von Humboldt, described the people, public life, history, and geography of Venezuela about 1804.

It is generally known that agriculture, cattle-raising, industry, and commerce increased considerably from 1800 to 1810. In other words, the immediate background of the revolution shows no economic depression. Although population as a whole probably increased, there are no certain figures. Estimates give the total population of all of Venezuela as between 700,000 and 800,000. One contemporary offers a figure in 1801 of 700,000 (one fifth white, two fifths free Negro, three tenths Negro, and the rest Indian). Alexander von Humboldt considered the number of slaves to be 62,000 (in a total population of 800,000). The creoles came to 200,000; European-born whites, 12-000. "Whence would result for the whole ancient Capitania-General of Caraccas the proportion of 0.51 mixed (mulattos, zambos, and mistizos), 0.25 Spanish Americans (creole whites), 0.15 Indians, 0.08 Negroes, and 0.01 Europeans." [5]

The Government and Society

The chief agency of government which spoke for local interests was the *cabildo*. The *cabildo* was the voice of the city, although it did not think, act, or move as the voice of the people. The *cabildo* of Caracas, and all other *cabildos* of the colony, represented the wealthier aristocracy of the city and suburbs. The locally born and raised well-to-do, or creoles, generally possessed large properties. They bought or inherited their *cabildo* posts, and conveyed their opinions and recommendations to the captain-general. The masses had little to do with the *cabildo* or with colonial politics in general. The captain-general and intendant noticed them even less.

At the birth of modern Venezuela, the society consisted of aristocrats, slaves, urban merchants, Indians, missionaries, and Negroes. The figures cited above indicate that about half the population was partly colored—*pardo* (*mestizo,* or mulatto). The Venezuelan *pardo* was not socially acceptable either to the creoles or to the European-born whites. The *pardos,* or colored, were descended from slaves. They

[5] *Ibid.,* pp. 117-18; see also Alexander von Humboldt, *Personal Narrative of Travels to the Equinoctial Regions of the New Continent during the Years 1799-1804,* Vol. VI (London, 1814-26), pp. 131-35.

specialized in manual crafts, such as carpentry, iron-work, black-smithing, tailoring, and the like. The absence of guilds worked to the *pardos'* advantage by allowing them to become journeymen without having to go through the prolonged vocational apprenticeship.

Pardos also formed the artisan and mechanic class of Venezuela. Some *pardos* also became small retail merchants. (Just as there were poor whites as well as wealthy whites, so were some of the *pardos* wealthier than the rest of their class.) Others were able to buy from the Crown petty titles of address and social status, as well as lesser civil posts—in spite of the established *limpieza de sangre* (race purity laws). This traffic enriched the Crown and pleased the ambitious *pardo* and his wife, but it aroused the racial dislike of the upper-class whites. In spite of all this, most of the Venezuelan *pardos* remained in a low-income, low-status category.

This was the social makeup of Venezuela at the time of the War for Independence. There was no class struggle among the different social groups. Individual issues and quarrels existed, but these did not grow into schisms, feuds, or rebellions. All life, even politics, was fairly quiet in the colony in 1810. The force for change arose from the outside: from Spain.

When Napoleon invaded Spain in 1808, exiled Venezuelans organized. The French takeover in Spain was designed to bring about an easy transfer of the Indies to France. But the French could not foresee that the *cabildo* of Caracas would take over the government, remove both captain-general and intendant, and seize executive power. The political Venezuelan revolution took place in April 1810. It drove out Vicente Emparán, last of the Spanish colonial governors of Venezuela, who had (according to Alexander von Humboldt) a "modern outlook" on the sciences.

The Independence Movement

The clash of interest between the emerging "patriot" and the established "tory" groups came out into the open on April 19, 1810, at the meeting between the Caracas *cabildo* and Captain-General Emparán. Press and public gossip had already aroused a good deal of notice and talk. Since 1808 there had been a newspaper in Caracas: the *Gazeta de Caracas*. Depending upon who controlled the city of

Caracas, the *Gazeta* was first republican in its point of view, then royalist, and finally republican again until 1821. *Gazeta de Caracas* confused and misled its readers by insisting that Napoleon would soon be overthrown. The French conquest of Spain as far down as Seville and the Austrian defeat at Wagram came as a terrible shock to Caracas. All the news of "victories" were lies after all. Venezuelans were more and more convinced that Spain was done for.

The truth of the Napoleonic victories cost Emparán his position and his influence. Even before that, the basic institutions of the city —*cabildo,* university, *audiencia,* and army—had developed an antipathy toward him. The news discredited and contradicted him. According to his own *Memoirs,* written in Philadelphia in June 1810 the patriots (some four or five hundred of them in the *cabildo* hall) argued that Spain had lost all. Not only was Spain unable to resist, but the mother country would now need still more money, supplies, and food from the Venezuelans. It did Emparán and the royalists no good to repeat the myth about Spanish resistance. At this point the *cabildo* colonials took his government from him, setting up their junta which "respected the rights and loyalties due to Fernando VII so far as it was compatible with the interim sovereignty of the people."

Only in Caracas was this turnover effective; the support of the provinces was necessary to make it universal. The new junta knew it and acted at once. Setting itself up as the supreme junta, Caracas defended itself for acting alone and invited the *cabildos* of the other provinces to a convention to form a new government. Some of the provinces supported the junta; others did not. Caracas abolished the *alcabala* (or sales tax) and the poll tax. It released from prison, for a more useful labor in society, those confined under the insidious charge of "vagrancy," and also reorganized the army to reward those soldiers who had helped the new government. In June 1810 the deputies met. They elected (under restricted, qualified, and indirect suffrage) the first popularly elected representative government in Latin America.

The Caracas junta then sent Colonel Simón Bolívar, Andrés Bello, and Luis López Méndez to Great Britain to get recognition and aid. Francisco de Miranda, who was in London at that time, offered the Caracas junta his services. When news came from Bogotá that a supreme junta had also been established there, Venezuela sent a patriot plenipotentiary to negotiate a treaty of federal union as well as friendship, leaving the door open to the admission of other colonies.

Francisco de Miranda returned to Caracas in January 1811, and a reluctant junta named him lieutenant-general. The wild demonstrations in his behalf when he rode into Caracas were in sharp and fatefully misleading contrast with the apathy which had greeted his attempted invasion of Venezuela in 1806. He could not see in 1811, nor in 1806, any omen which would foreshadow the coming twilight of his long career. A former general of France and a veteran soldier, Miranda at once set about drilling, organizing, and training the army which came under his command.

Civil troubles threatened. On March 2, 1811, the first general congress of the United Provinces of Venezuela met, dominated by twenty-four members from Caracas. That first congress abolished the Negro slave trade into and out of Venezuela.

The Rise of Simón Bolívar

Outside the congress, a patriotic pressure group had been formed with the returned Bolívar and Miranda as leaders. Enemies charged that the patriotic society was Masonic and some members of congress opposed it for being a Jacobin club. But the society survived and took up the rights of citizens as the constitutional basis of government. Propaganda on behalf of freedom and equality was circulated everywhere. The heat and enthusiasm of the topics attracted mass numbers from all classes. Meetings were open to all—even to women. Speakers denounced Spain; few openly defended the peninsula. They orated against tyranny, the commercial monopoly, corruption, taxes, and the despotism of Governor Emparán. The seeds of independence were already sown.

Venezuela declared its independence on July 5, 1811, when thirty-eight of the forty-four deputies voted to make Venezuela a free nation. The statement was preceded on July 1, 1811, by a Declaration of the Rights of the People in seven articles, and a Declaration of the Rights of Man in Society in twenty-seven articles. These also gave the duties of man in society and the duties of society to man. None of the three declarations mentioned slavery or the Negro as such.

Equality before the law and protection of individual liberty and moral rights were proclaimed. Miranda and others chose a national flag, selecting the colors yellow, blue, and red which he brought ashore with him in 1806 at his ill-fated liberation attempt. The government then named the sons of the patriot of 1797, José España, to carry the battle flags of Venezuela's first army. The Archbishop of Caracas gloried openly at how his Venezuelan church was taking its place among great national Catholic churches.

Royalist revolts at once greeted this event by opening ten bitter and bloody years of civil war. From 1811 to 1821, colonialism fought back at nationalism. Violence begot violence and the junta made use of General Miranda and Colonel Bolívar. Miranda, whose star rose for the first year, had thought of Bolívar as a "dangerous youth." For Bolívar, the glamor of Miranda's fame and European career wore off: all he could see was an old man. In spite of this rivalry, the government's program was both clear and successful. In December 1811 Venezuela had its first constitution.

The new constitution provided a three-man executive (Miranda was its vice-president). The clergy lost their *fueros* (privileges), and the colored people were given equality with all other citizens before the law by the repeal of all laws which imposed the *degradación civil* (civil degradation) upon them. The slave trade was abolished.

There is no doubt that the new constitution was a liberal and advanced document, but it was born under the shadows of Spanish determination to regain Venezuela. Under Domingo Monteverde, the Spaniards made a landing at royalist Coro and began their campaign to recapture Venezuela. Monteverde's marines were supposed to have stated that they would give no quarter. This might have been the origin of the war-to-the-death formula which spilled so much blood on the Venezuelan plains and cities during that deadly decade.

Then on March 26, 1812, Nature struck: a violent earthquake ruined Caracas and the other chief cities. Panic and mass hysteria heightened the feelings of sin, penance, and guilt among the populace as the terrible "act of God" smote the new patriots. The catastrophe had taken place on Holy Thursday, and the priests made the "significance" of all this very clear. "Even the most animated patriots practiced acts of ridiculous penance in order to ward off the anger of heaven," wrote a contemporary historian who witnessed the scene. But the royalist cause did not suffer. Guiana fell to the royalists when the patriots around Angostura fled in fright after the earthquake to the other side of the Orinoco. The quake was worth more than ten military victories to Monteverde, who now advanced on Caracas.

Blunders, disobedience, and personal ambitions marred the patriots' defense plans. At the end of April 1812 an alarmed executive and a desperate congress proclaimed Francisco de Miranda dictator, with absolute powers over the deteriorating situation. At his insistence, the congress also gave him military supremacy and the title *Generalissimo*.

But events went from bad to worse. The countryside was aflame with Negro slave revolts, religious fanaticism, and unexpected surrenders. Patriotic morale was generally low. Colonel Bolívar left for the seacoast and prepared to sail for Colombia. Miranda sought an armistice with Monteverde. Caracas was about to fall. The personal quarrel between Bolívar and Miranda gave a dramatic denouement to their country's fall: in July 1812 Bolívar had a hand in the arrest of Miranda. Others betrayed Miranda and turned him over to the Spaniards, who took him to Cadiz and imprisoned him in the dungeon where he died on July 14, 1816.

Simón Bolívar, who remained convinced that Miranda had betrayed the First Republic, spent the next few years fighting and losing in New Granada (now Colombia). Meantime, Monteverde restored the acts and machinery of Spanish monarchy in Venezuela. Royalists, Negro slaves, and religious extremists pounced upon those who stayed behind. Monteverde, who won the honorary title *Pacificador*, enjoyed full command over the country. He even prevented the restoration of the captain-general in order to assume total leadership. Venezuelans today view his acts as despotic, violent, cruel, and immoral, injuring property and persons throughout the colony. But others defend his acts as necessary for Spanish law and order. The Caracas *cabildo* went over to his side; so did other *cabildos*. On the other hand, any pledge of amnesty he had given Miranda before the armistice was forgotten, and Venezuela under Monteverde experienced a royalist reign of terror. For those few years before 1817, Monteverde and Spain were in the saddle again. Monteverde had done well: he had captured and sent to Spain that Miranda whom

Spain had been wanting to arrest since 1780. Little did he realize that he had made a bad trade: his letting Bolívar escape while seizing Miranda was only the result of thinking in terms of the past. The past was Miranda's, but the future was Bolívar's. Monteverde had guessed wrong.

Bolívar came back briefly to Caracas from 1813 to 1814 with the support of New Granada. He re-established civil and political liberties. Colombia, in making Bolívar a brigadier-general and allowing its troops to go with him into Venezuela, expected Bolívar to restore the same government in Caracas that had existed there when Monteverde overthrew it. Bolívar ignored the Colombian conditions. He accepted his popular acclaim and his new role of supreme military and political chief. Opposing any restoration of a congressional and federal system, Bolívar centralized the government. He only sought to introduce the idea of a Venezuelan union with New Granada.

Monteverde succeeded in getting both the free and slave *pardos* in southern Caracas province to rise up against the Bolivarian government and swear allegiance to Fernando VII. They committed outrages which, according to an early patriotic historian, "memory shudders at recalling and the pen refuses to describe the details." Thus began the historic but infamous "war to the death" between patriots and royalists. It was at this time that an enlistment in the patriotic forces changed the history of Venezuela and Latin America: the famed Antonio José de Sucre, Bolívar's chief and most trusted aide.

The New Nation

New men and names were replacing the old, and moving into the pages of history. Tomás Boves replaced Monteverde at the head of the royalists. The country seemed irrevocably divided into two enemy camps. The military enmity was bad enough, but the social struggles were even worse. Between Boves and Bolívar there was no rest until July 1814, when Bolívar ordered a retreat from Caracas. His aides demurred, feeling there was enough republican strength to defend the capital.

Meantime, changes had also taken place in Spain. Fernando VII, now restored to power, ordered death and imprisonment to anyone who had supported the cortes or even the regency. Absolutism in

Spain found a spearhead in Caracas. Bolívar made his exodus. Behind him, on the Venezuelan plains, was still another new name: the cavalry guerrilla chief, José Antonio Páez.

Thousands of civilians, including the sick and wounded, left Venezuela with Bolívar while loyal holding forces fought Boves in Caracas. The holding action only postponed total defeat. Bolívar left by sea, returning all the way to Cartagena whence he had started. He left Venezuela with accusations of betrayal hurled at him, just as he had hurled them at Miranda two years before. He left behind his estates, his revenues, and a good part of his reputation. Behind him also were military disasters, the annihilation of his trapped soldiers, and even the slaughter of civilians.

Bolívar crossed the sea to Jamaica. His famous "Letter from Jamaica" in 1815 did not mark the end of a career but announced instead the end of Spain and the renewal of the battle for nationalism and independence. Bolívar looked towards his homeland and saw signs of renewed resistance to Spain on the island of Margarita, in the easterly province of Guiana, and in the emerging leadership of Páez on the *llanos*. Then he knew that he had been wrong in attempting to reconquer Venezuela by coming in from the Andes and Colombia. He determined to land and invade eastern Venezuela. With luck he could then go west over the Andes and free Colombia. Factions in the eastern and Orinoco regions soon learned of Bolívar's plan; they began to unite and sent an emissary to recall him.

When Bolívar returned to Venezuela early in 1817, he established his operations in the Orinoco, capturing a base in Guayana, the river city of Angostura (now Ciudad Bolívar). For the next few years his work was military and political. His military activities were of a preparatory nature. He gathered his new forces. He incorporated the famous Foreign Legion (Irish, British, German, and French veterans of the Napoleonic Wars), calling it "the British Legion." He concentrated his first military efforts upon the strategy of going upriver to unite his infantry with the *llanero* cavalry of Páez. Then he planned to cross the Andes and liberate Bogotá, even before attempting to free his own native Caracas.

His political activities led to the re-establishment of a congress and a new form of government over that vast region. A second national congress of Venezuela had been called in Angostura in February 1819. Bolívar's political ideas were put to work at once. The "Letter from Jamaica" in 1815 was his first serious political pronouncement. His address to the congress in 1819 was his second. The Angostura meeting heard Bolívar's ideas for a government for Venezuela. Bolívar opposed federalism, or even a three-man executive, as a source of weakness and disunity. In short, he no longer believed in the government of 1811. Now he put himself on record for an hereditary senate, elected by the congress, to be composed of a first generation of liberators or men specially trained for that position. He called for laws guaranteeing civil liberties and endorsing his military actions in freeing the slaves.

Then he set out for the west, crossing the Andes and leaving the Angostura congress behind him. Under the guiding hand of the vice-president, Francisco Antonio Zea, congress drew up a fundamental charter for a new nation: Colombia, Venezuela, and Ecuador (with the Guianas as part of Venezuela). The military and political plans were a joint success. At Boyacá, in 1819, Bolívar opened the road to Bogotá; at Angostura the congressionalists almost opened the door to a new future.

In August Bolívar wrote to Zea from Bogotá:

> Boyacá, our most complete victory, which we have just gained, has decided the fate of the inhabitants of these regions. After destroying every branch of the King's Army, I moved rapidly to this capital attended by great numbers of men who vied with each other in their expressions of tenderest gratitude, and who, falling upon the scattered remnants of the enemy, cooperated actively in his final rout; themselves unarmed, they seized the enemy's arms and took a large number of prisoners. Your Excellency will find the details of this victory in the papers which I herein enclose.[6]

Bolívar then returned to Angostura. Not long after that, congress completed the Fundamental Law of the nation of New Granada. As we have seen, the Angostura Congress of 1819 created a nation of three departments: Cundinamarca (Colombia), Quito (Ecuador), and Caracas (Venezuela). But Venezuela was still in Spanish hands, and Bolívar soon returned to Caracas.

[6] Harold Burck, Jr. (ed.), *Selected Writings of Bolívar*, compiled by Vicente Lecuna and translated by Lewis Bertrand. Vol. I (New York, 1951), p. 205.

Events from the outside now helped rather than hindered. In late 1820 a revolt among Spanish liberals and armed forces in Spain compelled the royalists in Caracas to negotiate an armistice with Bolívar. Pablo Morillo, successor to Monteverde and Boves, resigned his command and went back to Spain. Mopping up the remaining royalists proved to be easy, and the Venezuelan War for Independence came to an end.

The government and congress moved from Angostura to Cúcuta (just inside the Colombian border). The Cúcuta congress repeated the action of the Angostura congress in creating the nation of Gran Colombia and formally adopted the new constitution. Bolívar was elected president, but he never stayed in Venezuela long enough to carry out the office. He was already engaged in his ambitious continental strategy to march all the way to Peru.

FOUR

A Nation and its Forces

To 1900

After Bolívar

Carlos Soublette, friend and biographer of Bolívar, was the real Venezuelan president of the New Granadan Confederation after 1821. Bolívar was out of the country. Soublette was soon replaced by José Páez. During the decade from 1821 to 1831, generals or successful military leaders had assumed charge of the several administrative-military provinces which made up the Venezuelan part of Gran Colombia. They were the first military *caudillos* of postwar Venezuela. It fell to them to reward their veterans with grants of public lands, abandoned properties, jobs, and economic opportunities. In a sense, these veterans became the new rich of Venezuela. With José Páez as their voice, they caused enough unrest to bring about the breakdown of the whole Bolivarian structure. Much of their political opposition was directed toward the government at Bogotá, rather than toward their own leaders at Caracas. By 1826 the deepening cracks revealed the dangerous pressures.

The *llanero* Páez led Venezuela into nationhood. The country bore much of his stamp throughout her later history. Páez had declared Venezuela an independent nation in 1829. Bolívar was really unable to stop the Caracas aristocrats and the *llaneros* from breaking loose. He was mortally ill and wasted. In July 1830 Bolívar learned that his self-sacrificing friend and aide, Antonio José de Sucre, had been

36

assassinated in an Andes pass. In Venezuela a large assembly of small men had declared the great man an outlaw. Bolívar had already been given a pension in Bogotá and asked to leave Colombia. When he died in December 1830 on the shore at Santa Marta, Colombia and Venezuela, under Páez, were ready to get along without Bolívar.

The Emerging Caudillo: The Páez Era

Because Bolívar was away from Venezuela more than he was there, and because his powerful and military associate, Páez, remained there all the time, it was no surprise that Páez rose to the top of Venezuelan national politics while Bolívar sank. Páez was also a military hero and patriot. Although Bolívar and Antonio José de Sucre were leading figures in the liberation of Latin America as a whole, Páez became the primary figure in the liberation of Venezuela.

Bolívar was the strong man and chief executive in a protracted nominal presidency from 1813 to 1830 when the country was being liberated. Páez was the Venezuelan strong man and *caudillo* in the national period from 1830 to 1863. He did not meet Bolívar until 1818, when Bolívar left Angostura to cross the plains on the way to the Andes. Páez, born of poor parents in 1790, came from a lower social class than Bolívar, Miranda, or the other creole leaders from Caracas. Most of these had been to Europe and America; Páez never even left the Venezuelan plains until after he became president. Illiterate until maturity, he is famous in Venezuela not only for his political role but also for his *Autobiografía*. The Páez *Autobiografía* does not compare in size, volume, or literary quality with the autobiographic letters of Miranda and Bolívar, but it has a more rugged, earthy voice.

Bolívar soon discovered in Páez the talents of both a political and guerrilla leader, but Páez had to wait a while before he could move from the local to the national stage. He started as military leader of Caracas province. He later moved into the political arena when the *cabildo* of Valencia and then that of Caracas called him to leadership. During 1826 and 1827 Páez argued for the separation of Venezuela from Colombia. For a while he kept his aim secret because he wanted no fight with Bolívar (who, in turn, wanted no fight with Páez). In 1829 the *cabildo* of Valencia gave Páez his chance: the citizens there urged separation from Colombia, and the Caracas aristocracy followed suit. In January, 1830, Páez—as supreme executive—called for elections for a separate Venezuelan congress, to meet at the anti-Colombian city of Valencia.

Unlike the contemporary Argentine *gaucho* leader, Juan Rosas, who moved from civilization to barbarism, Páez rose from barbarism to civilization. He joined the educated and propertied classes at Caracas through his friendship with Carlos Soublette and Dr. José Vargas, both good friends of Bolívar. Soublette, vice-president after 1822 and again after 1830, was acceptable to Venezuelan society. Vargas, who became president of Venezuela in 1835, was an executor of Bolívar's will. Vargas, who had studied in Europe, was a well-known medical man. A North American intellectual leader said at that time that Vargas was the first scientist after Thomas Jefferson to become president of an American country. At that time Venezuela was controlled by an oligarchy of related families. This aristocracy had been able to survive the destruction and disorders of the previous twenty years. Páez matched their qualities with his new landed wealth, his revolutionary fame, his personal popularity, and most of all, his power.

Páez' first term as president of the new Venezuela began in 1830. Under the constitution of that year Venezuela again tried to introduce a federal system. Each of thirteen provinces had a legislature and a governor. Governors were nominated by a provincial deputation but were appointed by the president. The third level of government consisted of the local cantons and municipalities. The justices of district courts and the supreme court were chosen for four-year terms and could be reappointed. The president's term was four years, and no president could serve two successive terms. Guarantees of freedom were given and the usual property restrictions upon suffrage were included. With its token federalism resting upon a provincial basis, the Venezuelan constitution of 1830 can be called "centro-federal," with a large allotment of power to the national government and to the executive branch.

The first term of President Páez expired in 1835. The fact is that not only was Páez a strong ruler, but he was also a well-liked political personality. He was succeeded by Vargas, who was highly regarded by many important people in society but was not so highly thought of by the generals and junior officers. The military tried to enlist the help of influential citizens of Caracas in repealing the constitution and launching a new government. They failed, and were accused of being supporters of Bolívar. Páez was able to restore order, but Vargas, who was returned to office, resigned. Carlos Soublette, on his return from Spain, finished out Vargas' term of office. Then Páez was elected for another term (from 1839 to 1843). After that, Carlos Soublette was elected president in his own right and governed from 1844 to 1848. Soublette, half French and half Venezuelan, had served close to Miranda, Bolívar, and Páez since 1811 and was a prominent and socially important conservative of that era.

At the outset of this long Páez era, Venezuela had come through the destruction and chaos of the War for Independence with about 800,000 people,[1] about the same total population as had been estimated by Humboldt back in 1804. This was a good recovery, considering the losses caused by the great earthquake, the slave uprisings, the violence of the *llaneros*, and the no-quarter and war-to-the-death orders of the military. Caracas had about 35,000 people at this time; Maracaibo, 18,000; and Valencia, 15,000.

This population still included about 15,000 slaves in 1840—all that were left after manumissions and slave uprisings. Slavery was expected to disappear gradually, since after 1821 all slaves' children were born free, although they had to work for a master until they were eighteen. The Negro and part-Negro population were scattered in different parts of the country, but the largest part continued to live near the coast or in Guayana.

Each parish was supposed to have one grammar school. There were *colegios* for secondary education in the capital of each of the thirteen provinces. The University of Caracas provided higher education and professional training.

Venezuela was open to other religions besides Roman Catholicism. Freedom of worship was established on February 17, 1834. Although

[1] Carl A. Gosselman, *Informes sobre los Estados Sudamericanos en los Años 1837 y 1838*. Magnus Morner (ed.) Biblioteca e Instituto de Estudios Ibero Americanos de la Escuela de Ciencias Economics (Stockholm, 1962). The original account is dated Caracas, October 12, 1838.

Roman Catholicism was the religion of the State, the clergy did not have—from Bolívar's time to Páez'—the religious powers which they enjoyed elsewhere (in Colombia, for example).

Except for the short-lived military insurrections, the Páez-Soublette era was generally liberal, prosperous, and interested in progress. The conservatives looked forward rather than backward. Those who were associated with Páez governed Venezuela with a good deal of intelligence and enlightenment. So much remained to be done after the poverty of the long colonial era and the stresses of the revolution that the conservative tolerance of education and liberal ideas seemed to face insurmountable obstacles.

Nevertheless, the general rule for the country was progress. Even the tax system was modernized, and the old colonial taxes—which many Latin American nations kept as sources of revenue—were abolished. The Venezuelan tax system no longer rested upon monopoly and privilege; there was greater freedom for economic activity and trade. Free trade had come a long way since the eighteenth century, but the Venezuelan planters, the Caracas merchants, and the Venezuelan treasury now drew great profits from foreign trade.

In its nearly twenty years of power, the Páez-Soublette group established a few schools in the municipalities (chiefly city schools), built roads, and in general undertook the combined work of reconstruction as well as new construction. The government's foreign credit was good, although it had delayed repayment on bonds. Swedish commercial observers who visited Venezuela at the time give a favorable account of stable economic conditions, active trade, and numerous signs of prosperity (although these were not distributed evenly among the classes). Carlos Soublette, veteran of the War for Independence, signed the Venezuelan-Spanish peace treaty of 1845. There was still a vast amount to do for the country: roads were lacking; most parishes did not have the schools they were promised; and a great economic gap existed between the capital and the countryside and among the different classes.

The Struggle Among Liberals

The most troublesome factor, however, was neither class tension nor economic rivalry; it was politics. Páez' control of power had lasted for almost a whole generation after Bolívar and independence. The time was right for another party. After a decade of unsuccessful and sporadic opposition, the so-called Liberal Party appeared in the 1840's.

New leaders and new family groups took over or clung to political power. Some succeeded in passing power from father to son, as though politics were a form of private property. Among the leaders of the Venezuelan liberals were the editor-journalist of *El Venezolano*, Antonio Leocadio Guzmán, and the former Marquis del Toro (now "civilianized" under the name Francisco Rodríguez). The Marquis was one of the wealthiest landowners of Venezuela, a country already known for its vast estates. He was a liberal and a patriot, the uncle of Bolívar's wife, and an early revolutionary with both Miranda and Bolívar (some said he had been a revolutionary even before 1810). The Marquis was the liberal link to principles of liberty and liberation in the first half of the nineteenth century. Guzmán was the link to the more materialistic and ambitious liberalism of the second half of the nineteenth century and the first half of the twentieth century. Liberalism had a political interest in power, patronage, and public works and an economic interest in loans, financing, bonds, and interest. Liberalism therefore did not always wish to be free from government; it also wanted to run the government.

Nevertheless, the general formulas of nineteenth century liberalism were also present in Venezuela. Guzmán, who was educated in Spain, was closer to the ideas of Páez than to those of Bolívar. He was a cabinet minister during Páez' first administration, and then returned to newspaper publishing, through which he made himself politically prominent. Guzmán found or created many issues which justified his liberalism; they put him in the forefront of argument over questions of the day. He wrote on universal suffrage for the illiterate and impoverished, and welcomed the proposed abolition of Negro slavery.[2] Although he had married into the upper classes, he identified himself with the defense of the lower classes and generally appealed to the downtrodden and to the *pardos*. Himself a creole, Guzmán was fully aware of the political potential among the *pardos*—a potential which had been periodically tapped.

[2] William D. Marsland and Amy C. Marsland, *Venezuela through its History* (New York, 1954), p. 184.

Guzmán was more demagogue than democrat. Even the liberals were uneasy as he carried arguments for their issues too far. He surely alarmed the upper classes. But his demagogic democracy carried him almost to the heights of Venezuelan politics. High society and journalism were not enough for Guzmán. In 1844 his ambition led him to become a candidate for the presidency. But the opposition from his handicaps and his enemies (from whom even Páez could not save him) proved insurmountable. Guzmán came all the way down the political scale: he was put into jail, where he was at least safe from violence. With Guzmán in involuntary semiretirement, the political "Establishment" was able to put General José Tadeo Monagas into the presidency.

The ruling families of Venezuela's national era had not really evolved very far politically since colonial days. At that time, they had controlled the public offices. In the national period, they needed the *llanero*, the strong man, to rule for them. The aristocracy of Caracas could no longer produce important leaders; it now got them from the interior. Like Páez, General José Monagas had come up from the Venezuelan *llanos*. He, too, wore the halo of the revolutionary patriot and hero. But, unlike Páez, Monagas identified himself with the liberals, turning against those who had first elected him. He had great personal ambitions and wanted no advice. Monagas, viewed historically, sketched in the outline of the nineteenth century Venezuelan *caudillo*. In fact, he cast the dark shadow of all country-born dictators well ahead of him, even into the twentieth century.

First, Monagas strengthened his personal hold over the army. He dominated the cabinet and appointed weak Liberal ministers who did not oppose his personally staffing government positions. The showdown between the executive and legislative branches came soon after: Monagas overpowered congress. Congress made a bold but futile attempt to impeach him, but in 1848 he countered with a hard blow at individual congressmen and destroyed the independence of the legislative body. He even turned upon the venerable Páez in 1850 and sent him into exile. The Monagas family (his brother José Gregorio was president from 1851 to 1855 and José Tadeo resumed the presidency in 1855) were on their way to starting their own *caudillo* oligarchy in Venezuela.

Monagas also made good use of Guzmán, naming him vice-president and minister of the interior. He needed Guzmán to win the support of the press and the masses, and thus to supplement his own military and political power.

As president, Monagas made few changes and no improvements. The two Monagas brothers together did very little for Venezuelan society, but a great deal for themselves and their supporters. Oddly enough, however, the administration of José Gregorio must be given credit for the final emancipation of the slaves in Venezuela in 1854. (Abolition had long been promised, but since it was based upon the principle of compensation for the slaveowners, the government's purchase of the slaves' freedom had to wait until sufficient funds were available.) This was the most liberal achievement of the Monagas brothers. It was also almost their last.

When José Tadeo, convinced of his great powers, tried to change the constitution in 1857 to permit him to succeed himself, he led the way to his own overthrow. In spite of the wedge he tried to drive between liberals and conservatives, the issue inspired enough unity between the two groups to bring about his downfall. Even getting rid of Monagas provoked a crisis: a mob threatened the French Embassy, where he had sought refuge. Monagas was finally able to get out of the country and remained in exile for a decade.

After his departure, however, civil war ensued in Venezuela. The War of Federation lasted for five years. It represented a fight between strong-minded bosses such as Monagas and Páez (who had returned from New York to become dictator of Venezuela between 1861 and 1863), and also retained aspects of the clash of ideas and platforms between liberals and conservatives. The conflict drew upon factions within the army and the *llaneros*. Clans, power-seekers, merchants, landowners, plainsmen, and troublemakers all chose the sides they hoped would win.

The War of Federation was also the expression of a serious and historic difference between the centralists and the federalists. Since the time of Bolívar, Venezuelan centralism had always meant the rule of the government at Caracas. Federation or federalism stood for states' rights or the equality of the provinces with respect to any central government. It meant that Caracas should distribute tax income and customs revenue for roads, schools, and the advantages of the political-social elite in the provinces. Instead, Caracas kept these funds for her own continued advances. It was important for Caracas to build national income, increase foreign credit, and repay foreign debts. But it was also important, for the total growth of the nation, that the development of interior towns, estates, and provinces be accelerated and that their living standards, literacy levels, and cultural advantages be brought closer to those of the capital. All along the coast were cities and towns (Coro, Maracaibo, and Cumaná)—as old as Caracas and even more favorably located for trade and development—whose progress was hindered in favor of the vested interests of merchants, foreigners, and politicians living in Caracas.

Centralism did not have the political popularity and majority to govern Venezuela. Although the "big city" had money, culture, and power, it did not have the support of the raw country folk which the provinces of the interior could summon. Only one man from the capital—Bolívar—was able to maintain a centralized government by virtue of his own popularity and military power and the crisis of war. Bolívar was born a *caraqueño* and remained one politically, balancing his social graces and aristocracy with the campaign life of a soldier. In the end, Caracas rejected him. Páez, the self-taught and self-made *mestizo* from the prairies, forced upon the oligarchy of planters, merchants, and centralists in Caracas the realization that their conservative centralism would have to provide for the provinces. After the "centro-federalism" of Páez came the liberal era and the reawakening of provincial and regional dissatisfactions. Venezuelan nationalism had to embrace more than Caracas alone.

The Venezuelan Liberal Party, unlike the Colombian Liberal Party, did not get bogged down in the doctrinaire, intellectual concern for freedom, the separation of church and State, and the rights of man. It is true that some voices were raised for human liberty and equality, but on the whole liberalism in Venezuela was not the sweeping predemocratic force that altered the nature of the nation, as it was in Colombia, Mexico, Chile, and Argentina.

Liberalism in Venezuela during the nineteenth century provided an outlet for provincial federalism and a demogogic excuse for opportunistic *caudillos*. (The Monagas, for example, were Liberals.) Nevertheless, the familiar, serious, and patriotic aims of genuine liberalism did appear. They stayed alive, being permitted to whisper Venezuela's needs in the face of the triumphant shouts of *caudillismo, personalismo,* family oligarchies, and political dynasties. Those who boasted that they were liberal went over to the cause of federalism during the civil war. For some reason, federalism and not centralism had the magic quality attached to equality and liberty: it attracted the believers in universal suffrage, provincial equality, and a stronger congress. It had no social program, however. Federalism had a liberal aura, but not a real liberal basis.

Corruption, brutality, indecision, and deception dragged out the Venezuelan civil war. The liberal-federal pressure was strong. Even the old veteran Páez, who had imposed a dictatorship on his return, was no longer able to wield power. He could not beat the liberal-federal "rebels"; the provinces had by this time forgotten the old man of the *llanos,* who was now civilized. His political career drew to a close. He had to make way for others, members of a new generation who had not fought in the War for Independence or known Bolívar. Páez went back to New York for good.

The other side of liberal-federalism was manifest in those provinces whose local bosses could not be controlled by Caracas. The national government was beginning to have its own troubles with financial chicanery and the activities of pressure groups. The *jefes politicos* out in the provinces, each one with the private ambition of becoming governor, stirred up troubles which were hard to calm down. Paradoxically, they were also probably the best source of law and order, since they put each other out of the way by fighting and through assassination. They showed the worst possible side of regional-federalism—near-anarchy—which convinced urbane Caracas that the interior was uncouth and uncivilized. Caracas identified the provinces and the rural regions with an eternal feudal disorder. On the economic side, although Caracas controlled the income from customs, the provinces hoped for renewal of the old Spanish inland customs (*aduana seca*) or the local sales tax (*alcabala*). But this would have disrupted internal trade and prevented the rise of a national market which Caracas could then command.

Disorder piled on disorder. If it was possible, Venezuela deteriorated. The Monagas clan reappeared in 1868 and broke out into revolution. The Monagas clan had managed to work out a liberal-conservative front which called itself the "Blues." They captured Caracas. Their opponents, the "Yellows," were unable to stop the Monagas. Those terms, *Blue* for conservative and *Yellow* for liberals, were first used as popular labels at the beginning of that decade, even though the political platform each described was not very clearly distinguishable from the other. Many not only mixed allegiances but also blended the two colors. These groups were far from being political parties; they had a more dashing and probably more feudal character. José Tadeo Monagas died unexpectedly in 1868, leaving the presidency vacant. His son, Ruperto Monagas, stepped in promptly to claim his dynastic inheritance and keep the Monagas family in power. He almost succeeded, but a new rival appeared at this time: Antonio Guzmán Blanco.

The Guzmán Blanco Era

The Guzmán clan now decided the fate and politics of Venezuela. Old Antonio Leocadio Guzmán, the journalist, politician, and man of the people, had married into the Blanco family, members of the Caracas upper class. In 1828 his son, Antonio Guzmán Blanco, was born. Nurtured amid politics and intrigue, Guzmán Blanco achieved power in Venezuela after 1863, and governed as president from 1870 to 1888. The Guzmán dynasty, which had failed to elect the father as president, now ruled Venezuela through the son.

The Guzmán Blanco era began when young Guzmán Blanco, combining his own talents with the continued influence of his father, joined forces with the *caudillos* of the provinces, organizing them and acting as the spokesman for their provincial protests, grievances, and ambitions. In addition to this source of political strength, Guzmán Blanco was favored by the government with a key economic and financial position: he was appointed to negotiate loans and interest rates with the powerful London bankers. In negotiating the loan of 1870, Guzmán Blanco made (it has been estimated) his own profit of £176,000. The face amount of the loan to Venezuela was £1,500,-000; the net amount which arrived in Caracas (after deduction of previous obligations) was £200,000. But the country remained charged with the face amount. After returning to Venezuela, young Guzmán Blanco moved easily into financial posts in the government.[3]

[3] *Ibid.*, pp. 197-98.

Antonio Guzmán Blanco brought Venezuela out of civil war and competitive *caudillismo* into a forced prosperity and a one-*caudillo* rule. Beginning as a liberal, he broke with the liberal-conservative front when it seemed to be victorious. Guzmán Blanco launched his new career as the leader of generals, although he was not a soldier. He entered Caracas as a victor in April 1870, at the head of a movement called *Regeneración* (Regeneration). He became president for a first term of almost eight years, from 1870 to 1877. Guzmán Blanco —modern, a Mason, and a lover of things European—was well aware of Venezuelan problems and needs. And he brought to his task a new, modern approach.

Guzmán Blanco, prototype of all Venezuelan *caudillos,* brought Venezuela down to the end of the nineteenth century. He is the *Caudillo* of George Wise's book of that name. No doubt exists about the regeneration and reconstruction effected under his long rule. The Guzmán Blanco era was a period of considerable material development. Venezuela and Venezuelans made money. Considerable funds were allocated to public works and the construction of railways, piers, and roads. Both contracts and profits were extensive. At the same time, Guzmán Blanco launched the effort to start the long road toward universal education by equipping municipal grammar schools and *colegios.* It was but a drop in the bucket of widespread ignorance and illiteracy, to be sure, but it was a beginning. A practical politician, Guzmán Blanco also created the modern city of Caracas as the center of a network of roads, ports, and telegraphic communications.

Although modern technology and public works received most of his attention, Guzmán Blanco also devoted some of his practical liberalism to Venezuela's Church-State relations. In fact, this was the area of his major reform. He directed the reform against the Church, which he regulated firmly. He reasserted civil supervision over such matters as birth and marriage, which up the Church had controlled alone. Guzmán Blanco, a Grand Master of Venezuelan Masonry, pushed the Church back from public and political life.

When Guzmán Blanco stepped down to live out his days in the society and gaiety of Paris, General Joaquin Crespo followed him into presidential office and power. Crespo's otherwise colorless administration was raised to fame by the Venezuela boundary dispute with British Guiana. The Venezuelan claim to both sides of the Orinoco was accompanied by an interest in gold and precious stones rumored to be found there. The pressure applied by the United States led to an arbitration of the dispute. In 1962, the matter was reopened by a protest against the earlier settlement, with Venezuela now opposing the claims made by the present government of British Guiana. The dispute has not yet been settled.

FIVE

EARLY TWENTIETH-CENTURY HISTORY

The Gómez Era

Cipriano Castro, who followed Crespo as president of Venezuela, opened the country to the twentieth century. For the next half-century, the country seemed destined to continue along lines laid out in the preceding century: economic gains, political "bossism," and widespread illiteracy. Liberalism came to an end and was replaced by a rural and provincial conservatism. The relations of Caracas to the countryside underwent a most important change: strangers, not natives, came in to the capital and ran both Caracas and the country. Castro was the first of almost two generations of Andean, country-born *caudillos*. The Andeans took over the city, moved in upon civilized life and society, and came to practical terms with Caracas. The new twentieth-century *caudillo* derived from the Andean cattleman and rancher, just as the nineteenth century Páez and some of his successors derived from the southern plains.

Still wanting to be known as "liberals," the new leaders guided Venezuela along old lines. Castro's aide was the future "tyrant of the Andes," Juan Vicente Gómez. He became vice-president under Castro, looking out at the world he was soon to dominate himself. Gómez himself assumed the presidency and dictatorship in 1908. Castro proved small in his banality and venal material rule. Gómez towered over the first quarter of the twentieth century because he had a powerful political fist and because he presided over the vast outpouring of Venezuelan petroleum.

Little is notable in the ten years of Castro's rule, but much went on that was unnoticed. Probably the most effective area of his leadership was in the international field. He showed more energy in patriotics, nationalism, and flag-waving than in any serious domestic legislation, reform, or progress. The best-known incident was the Venezuela Debt controversy of 1902, which involved Germany, Italy, and England at first and then widened to include the United States (concerned about possible aggression against Venezuela). It was finally brought to the International Tribunal at the Hague in 1906, and Venezuela won. This was a great moral victory for Castro and brought him a great deal of popularity. This otherwise small, unimpressive figure became a hero whose exploits concealed his peculations and tyranny. He had come a long way in the international diplomacy—a far cry from his rural beginnings in the Andes.

One long-range change was the political-geographic shift from Caracas to the Andes. Castro was a new chieftain, a cattleman from ranching country in the far west. He and Gómez represented the so-called Táchira dynasty. They both came from Táchira, the extreme western state right on the Andes. Both rose through local politics, developing into officials and state governors. For the next half-century (in fact, until 1945), these westerners kept the balance of political power in the Andes. The old nineteenth century Blues and Yellows now faded away as the new *politicos* made their own sectional terms.[1]

There were some elements of social revolution in this political shift, but not fundamental ones. A devoted rural population followed Castro and Gómez from Táchira all the way to Caracas. In some ways, the country conquered the city. In the future, Caracas intellectuals, conservatives, and leaders had to prove a need for their services in government. The rising income from oil had reduced the politican's dependency upon real estate, land, and the other historic forms of the wealth of the urban oligarchy. Economic patterns as well as political scenes were changing in Venezuela. Táchira proved an obstacle to progressive liberalism, democracy, enlightened conservatism, and

[1] John E. Fagg, *Latin America: A General History* (New York, 1963), p. 816.

Marxism. Democracy and Marxism hardly existed in early twentieth century Venezuela. Few were ready to think along such lines.

After 1900 the cattle and ranching *caudillo* became the primary political power of Venezuela; he supplied the substance and direction for the issues of the day. Andean conservatism—hidebound, strong, and determined—was based upon closed folkways rather than upon open democracy. It was certainly nonintellectual. The political terms it laid down were indeed harsh, one-sided, and not open to debate. After a century's struggle over federalism, liberty, and greater regional expression, there emerged just the opposite: a strong, central power and one-man rule.

The income and profits of the new *caudillo* were enormous. The great day of oil had dawned in Venezuela. Gómez' long terms of office and power coincided with the oil industry's first impact on Venezuelan economics and politics. Gómez favored that great change. In one sense, Gómez led Venezuelans into the modern world economically while holding the country back politically. He himself moved about easily in civilized Caracas. He had shrewd and calculating instincts which allowed him to negotiate with the wisest lawyers, bankers, and diplomats. Yet the fact is that Gómez never wanted to throw off or grow out of the feudal values and society from which he came. He governed Venezuela as though it were his fief. He was the harsh patrón or the respected *compadre* of the people. The paternalism contained in these two sociopolitical terms was evident in Venezuela as it behaved under his "old-fashioned" ways. Gómez was the patronizing *señor* of a population of vassals. Education had not created citizens in Venezuela and political power prevented them from creating themselves.

But this man from the Andes knew very well how to control the big city, Caracas. He came out of the west to save the coffeegrowers, traders, landowners, professionals, and propertied leaders of Caracas society from being economically eaten up by civil war, decline in money values, and loss of property. He appeared just at the same time that the enormous oil riches increased Venezuelan credits, resources, and provided interest for bankers.

The political rivalry and concealed jealousy between Castro and Gómez worked very well for Gómez, who played his game shrewdly and patiently. His celebrated intrigues and betrayals bore fruit in

1908, when he seized power. Castro's illness and departure for Europe gave Gómez his chance.

As the unexpected heir to the Liberal Party of the nineteenth century and the beneficiary of Bolívar's struggle to create the Venezuelan nation, Gómez brought his semiliterate and loyal *andinos* to power with him. Nor must it be thought that they came with muddy boots to soil the capital; they adapted very well to the charms of the city and acquired the veneer of personal pride, political office, and the gayer habits of the town. At the same time, Gómez had the peculiar power to win over intellectuals—or at least some of them. To him they were but more office-seekers, and he treated them accordingly. Office-seekers flocked to Caracas. Gómez appointed relatives by the hundred. His family surrounded him in high offices and low. Thousands of others were spurned, put into jails, exiled, or cruelly mistreated. These were his critics, his enemies, his opposition, who did not belong to his clan. Gómez brought in an era of fascism, but he had no program or blueprint for fascism, no theory of society or class. He merely understood and handled the tools of personal power.

Money, rather than any philosophy about mass movements, modern nationalism or the nation-State, talked for Gómez.[2] He could not have been what he turned out to be within the economic pattern of the old Venezuela. He fell heir to a source of money which allowed him to "own" the old Venezuela and play a tyrant's politics without any challenge. His oil politics provided Venezuela and Gómez himself with vast revenues which he used to perpetuate his control as well as to provide a national prosperity. Venezuela's government was really well off under Gómez: foreign trade increased and a regular surplus was established; credit was very well sustained by payment of interest; ample funds became available for high salaries, graft, fancy public works, and the ever-increasing personal and family wealth of Gómez. Only the poor remained poor. The government's wealth and Gómez' wealth did little or nothing to redeem the city and country poor. Poverty remained chronic long after Gómez was gone. Individuals in the lower classes who played his politics were generously rewarded and climbed up the social scale, but Gómez never did anything with the vast wealth of Venezuela to eradicate poverty, illiteracy, malnutrition, slums, and immorality.

[2] John Lavin, A *Halo for Gómez* (New York, 1954), Chap. 3.

Unwilling to share control of Venezuela with any other power, Gómez differed with the procedure used by Colombia. He continued the liberalism of Guzmán Blanco and turned down a concordat with the Vatican. He paid no attention to the illiteracy of so many others besides himself and built far more public structures and city hotels than schools. When he was finished with his feudal-family reign, Venezuela looked good to the tourist but not to the inhabitant. The human resources of the country were underdeveloped, and because he dealt harshly with criticism, opposition, and proposals for reform, they remained so. Gómez was generous only toward the country's nonhuman resources; for oil promotion, sale, income, and prospecting, he did more than anyone might have expected.

The Uses of Oil

In 1914 the first oil was pumped from Lake Maracaibo, where Spain had established Venezuela's earliest settlement. Shrewd enough to value private property himself, Gómez understood the incentive provided by private enterprise. He refrained from any socialistic measures, offering the major companies concessions and leases and securing for himself and the Venezuelan treasury substantial royalties and taxes. This fundamental policy—based on nonexpropriation and nonnationalization—has continued to the present. Only the government's share of the oil royalties has increased, but private exploitation and development continue. From 1910 to 1935, Gómez cultivated the foreign oil companies as much as they cultivated him. British Shell, North American Standard, Creole, Gulf, and Texas operated in Venezuela.

The transformation of the country into an oil-based society really began in the 1920's, and is still going on. The great boom which transformed Maracaibo began, after 1937, to lead to oil discovery and exploitation in eastern Venezuela. Gómez was the first to appreciate the importance of this source of national wealth.[3] He let the foreigners extract the oil, sell it, and pay him for the privilege. Gómez started in 1920 with a small royalty; this attracted the companies. Today, the Venezuelan government asks for and gets more than

[3] Arthur P. Whitaker, *The United States and South America: The Northern Republics.* American Foreign Policy Library (Cambridge, Mass., 1948), pp. 55, 60-61.

49 per cent of profits. Venezuela has learned how oil provides income to support many state functions and eases the tax burdens on other types of wealth.

When oil was first discovered in the country and geologists figured Venezuela to be almost one vast underground resrvoir of oil, Venezuela rejoiced at the wealth in prospect. All through the Caribbean —in Colombia, Cuba, Central America, and Venezuela—the dawn of the era of prosperity coincided with the stir of Communism, strikes, radicalism, and student demonstrations. Gómez was unconcerned about the turmoil that broke out in Venezuela: he jailed hundreds of students and the junior army officers who tried to revolt. Gómez continued to rule in his fashion—making money and using strongarm controls—unconcerned about social change, political democracy, or constitutional expression.

Never married (a moot point), Gómez identified Venezuela and his presidency with his person and his progeny. He *was* the nation. The Gómez political family covered the country and held all the most lucrative jobs. Still, there was enough money left over to support the army of politicians, to build bridges and roads, and to fill private coffers. The prosperity withstood the challenge extended by radicals, students, and early Communists. But outside of Venezuela repression was severe.

The Rise of the Left

The year 1928 was an historic one in the Caribbean. In that year, Gustavo Machado, now the leader of the Venezuelan Communist Party, was one of those who felt the heavy fist of Gómez. Jorge E. Gaitán, a Colombian leftist, led a strike against the United Fruit Company. Julio Mella, the young Cuban Communist, and Sandino in Nicaragua, stimulated leftist agitation. Colombia, Nicaragua, and Cuba heard the roll of the working class drums, but the bland, terrible Old Man of Venezuela paid no attention and used the same old methods that had worked for him before.

The University of Caracas students launched their strike with an unexpected and unannounced speech which attacked the government. It was made in the middle of Student Week—a time devoted not to serious thought or politics but to festive and spirited collegian affairs. The students had paraded to the National Pantheon to lay a wreath at the tomb of the National Liberator. There, the comparison of Bolívar with Gómez was too tempting and too obvious a topic.

The student strike of February 1928 at the Central University of Caracas brought into the limelight two students who were to become the leaders of a new generation: Jóvito Villalba and Rómulo Betancourt. Today, they are the political leaders of Venezuela.

Villalba was arrested and jailed. His fellow-students protested and demanded his freedom and that of the other students who had been arrested with him. The University student body, the Federación de Estudiantes, wired their protest to Gómez. More students were arrested and taken away. The student arrests led to further demonstrations, the heightening of anti-Gómez feelings, and police action. The peak was reached some weeks later, in April, when some junior officers plotted with the students and intellectuals to overthrow the *caudillo*. For a brief moment, violence, in the form of an angry mob, took over a public building, but loyal troops and senior officers stifled it by gunfire. The political might of the dictator prevailed: large numbers of students and junior officers were imprisoned; others were put to hard labor; still others were exiled.

Gómez had kept the old constitution under which he had been elected for several seven-year terms. He instituted one restricting procedure: hereafter, the congress, not the public, was to elect the president. The indirect system worked well for Gómez. His last election was in 1922. The next presidential elections were due in 1929. The student-officer revolt of 1928 had opened the way to other revolutionary efforts. None of them were successful, but they kept Gómez' police and army on the alert throughout the election year.

Gómez was old and sick. At seventy, he had five more years of life and political power ahead of him. Partly because he was not well, partly because he was clever, he went through the motions of offering his resignation to congress in 1929, and decided not to run. He brought congressmen to Maracay to hear his farewell—his intention to leave the sword and decree and retire to the plow and agriculture. The cattleman- and farmer-image remained part of his simple and humble appearance; but he had enormous strength, will, and—of course—wealth. He had a puppet judge elected by congress; he lasted two years. Then congress went again to Gómez to get him to return to the presidency, which he did in 1931.

The loyalty of congress was assured through intimidation and patronage; but the army, the police, officeholders, journalists, and intellectuals continued to run the country for him. The long shadow of
Gómez as tyrant darkened the days of that depression decade 1930-40.
It was the shadow of the longest dictatorship in Latin America, but
it had to end. Nature, not man, decided Venezuela's fate in 1935,
as it had in 1812. The earthquake of 1812 was more disastrous than
the political earthquake that followed the death of Gómez in December 1935, but the latter had a longer chain reaction.

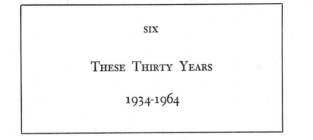

SIX

THESE THIRTY YEARS

1934-1964

After Gómez: Contreras and Medina

It took a little while for the new Venezuela to adjust to
the changed situation. While they were thus unready, imprisoned or
in exile, the old guard continued along the established way. The
Táchira clique continued to hold the presidency under Eleazar López
Contreras, who became acting president in 1935. Contreras, loyal to
Gómez and his Minister of War, dated his career from as far back
as the early days of both Castro and Gómez. He was a member of
the Gómez inner group and undoubtedly seemed tied to the spirit
of the previous era.

Contreras was, on the whole, a surprise. He began by allowing public expressions of violence and hostility toward the memory and pic-
tures of Gómez. He abolished censorship, released political prisoners,
and permitted exiles to return. Venezuela acquired freedoms in that
first year which had been denied her citizens for many years. In place
of personalist government, group ideas again appeared and the students' federation of 1928 was reactivated in 1935 and 1936. Jóvito
Villalba again came to the foreground. Demonstrations and strikes,
parades and protests marked the new political scene.

Contreras went on to lay the basis for reform in public education.
He stimulated the rising working class as well as students and returned intellectuals. The government adopted advanced labor legislation. The high-sounding laws included minimum wages, the right

to organize and strike, unemployment insurance, and supervision of working conditions. But it was apparent that Contreras had no intention of going "left." He denounced agitation and "communism" in labor and among students. Matters became clearer in 1936 when Congress met and elected Contreras president in his own legal right.[1]

Congress and the president passed a Public Order law, which made clear the government's intention of curbing demonstrations and strikes. The government resisted a month-long strike for rights and liberties. Police powers were resumed; no more revolts took place. As order and prosperity returned, politics began to change. The students' federation split into many factions. Under Villalba, Rómulo Betancourt, and various Catholic leaders, a number of new parties and political organizations were born—some of which still exist. The propertied groups created the Union Nacional Republicana; the predecessor of the Christian Democratic party was formed; and Betancourt headed the forerunner of Acción Democrática.

But the general strike left hard feelings in government. Radical parties and movements were suppressed and soon all opposition parties were put down as Contreras finished out his term as a typical Venezuelan strong man. Nevertheless, he had revived political activity. Political ideas were again in the air and on the march, even if only underground.

The Táchira clique continued to maintain control of the presidency. When Contreras' term expired in 1941, he chose his own successor: General Isaias Medina Angarita, his minister of war, who was also from Táchira. Since the congress and not the public was the electing body, it was a foregone conclusion that Medina would be the choice. His opponent in 1941 was Rómulo Gallegos, former minister of education, famous novelist, and future president. Gallegos was supported —in fact, proposed—by Betancourt, whose Acción Democrática had already been formed.

President Medina held office from 1941 to 1945. The acute reign of terror established under Gómez had been considerably eased under Contreras. The next step was to restore liberties and make changes. President Medina allowed political parties to function again. He took

[1] William D. Marsland and Amy C. Marsland, *Venezuela Through its History* (New York, 1954), p. 250.

under consideration the controversial religious bill which would have allowed the government to secularize religious schools—an issue which aroused much argument and split many groups. Medina, in a bold move, granted suffrage to women. He also granted freedom of speech and the press, restoring Venezuelan journalism and intellectualism to a position of influence. His cabinet was more nearly representative than congress and different views were expressed there. In 1943, however, a new congress came in, with views more typical of the day. Medina allowed free elections and the new parties took part in the campaign. It was Medina who added to and gave real meaning to labor laws and social security legislation. He proposed the agrarian reforms and land redistributions which have now become the accepted platform in Venezuela among reforming parties. At the same time, he showed how to finance social changes by the law of 1943, the model for the present one, which provided for higher royalties and taxes on oil profits without nationalizing the foreign companies.

By 1946, another presidential election year, the several parties wanted to change the constitution. To add to the confusion, Contreras reappeared to take a hand in the naming of the president. Contreras and Medina, although both members of the Táchira group, soon broke. The group had a left and right, a progressive wing and a conservative one. Contreras led the conservative-military wing; Medina was more progressive and liberal. Medina also had more prestige: he had led Venezuela through World War II after declaring war upon the Axis in 1945, and then had brought the country into the United Nations. But the government's connection with the military and the entry into the war put the military back into the political picture. On October 18, 1945 an officers' revolt broke out, overthrowing President Medina.

Medina surrendered to a young officer named Major Marcos Pérez Jiménez. Then the major left the political foreground to permit Betancourt to take over as provisional president. By that time Acción Democrática had already come out for mild socialism, the taxation of excess profits, the unionization of workers, and the division of land. Both the military and the party agreed upon universal suffrage and popular elections. The Revolution of 1945 became one of the milestones of modern Venezuela. The alliance between the revolutionary

officers and the left-of-center Acción Democrática, between the former
students of 1928 and the new military of 1945, was first marked by
their joint participation on a *junta revolucionaria*.

Acción Democrática and the Events of 1945

The provisional head of the junta was Betancourt. Other members
were Luis B. Prieto, editor of the important periodical *Política*. Another early member was Raúl Leoni, victorious candidate in the presidential elections of 1963 (the Acción Democrática nominee and successor to Betancourt). Many democratic steps were taken; the junta
lined itself up on the international political scene by breaking relations with Franco's Spain and Trujillo's Dominican Republic. The
trend was clearly antifascist and prodemocratic. The Communist
Party came alive again in Venezuela after 1945, but Acción Democrática, a party whose political nature was "left of the British Labor-
ites and right of the Communists," brought a new program and a
modern leader to Venezuela's nationalism and liberalism.[2]

The Venezuelan revolution of 1945 took many other forms. The
government opened the country to immigration from Europe. It
turned away from excessive free enterprise and economic liberalism by
aiding, regulating, and intervening in the economy. Land-reform proj-
ects and political democracy were discussed and promoted. The oil-
workers' union, largest in the country, and already with strong social
leanings, supported Acción Democrática and the junta in exchange
for the great social gains which the government made possible. Another step forward was the constitution of 1947. As nonrevolutionary
governments had already discovered, the heavy tax on oil profits could
finance most of Venezuela's activities (even reforms). Since the government would not kill the goose that laid the golden egg, there were
no provisions for nationalization either in the constitution or in political platforms. Acción Democrática had no intention of nationalizing
oil. The future seemed assured for good government and gradual,
evolutionary, social change.[3]

[2] *Ibid.*, pp. 258-60.
[3] Stanley J. Serxner, *Acción Democrática of Venezuela: Its Origin and Development.* Latin American Monographs, 9 (Gainesville, 1959), pp. 8-22.

Return to the Military

The president they elected, the famed novelist Rómulo Gallegos, lasted only nine months. Inaugurated in February 1948 to carry forward the improvements begun by the revolutionary junta, the unlucky Gallegos never had a chance. The civilian-intellectual was overthrown by the unelected: the army. In November 1948 the same army officers of the governing wing of the junta staged a coup. The first stage of political education in Venezuela was over. The army officers' cooperation with Acción Democrática had been deceptive. They could not accept the promises, made in public, to socialize the land for the Venezuelan peasants or to lead the workers towards Venezuelan socialism. Even more dangerous to them—as members of a profession rather than a social class—was the new proposal, typical of revolutionary movements of our times, that the army and its officers be reduced in size and influence and replaced by workers' and peasants' militias. The idea of trade union battalions and *campesino* rifles was an antimilitary revolution in itself. It was stopped.

Marcos Pérez Jiménez came forward again. This time his military regime governed Venezuela from 1950 to 1958. It was abruptly ended by public restlessness and by the overthrow of his dictatorship in 1958. Extradited in 1963 from his exile in the United States to face trial for his personal graft and peculation, Pérez Jiménez was a hard but luxury-loving dictator. Coming from Táchira, and part of the regional and military-political clique in control of national power for so long, Pérez Jiménez was much more transparent than either Gómez or Contreras. He never had the mass respect and deference that Gómez was able to command. Under Pérez Jiménez the machinery of the dictatorship shifted openly and defiantly to the military. Once again the soldiers and military stunted Venezuela's political and constitutional growth.

Postwar prosperity favored and helped the Pérez Jiménez regime. It was very well off economically, even if it was poverty-stricken politically. The oil profits that went abroad spoke louder than the voices of Gallegos and Betancourt, who were also abroad, but in exile. High wages, the usual Venezuelan public works programs, profits, and the modernization of Caracas poured money into many pockets. It was an era of show and wealth for the new rich as well as the old rich. But there was also much political bitterness around, as well as real social distress and abject poverty. It was under Pérez Jiménez that the great mineral wealth of the eastern states of Venezuela began to attract foreign companies into Venezuela, producing a vast wealth in addition to that produced by oil.

Such a situation fooled Pérez Jiménez into thinking that he could get an even stronger government by providing a more dictatorial constitution. He gained this end by a plebiscite in 1957. A few months later, beginning in January 1958, he paid for this excess of power: a series of demonstrations and actions, backed by high military officers, put Pérez Jiménez out of office.

Return to Acción Democrática

Wolfgang Larrazábal, one of the admirals of the regime, took over the junta which replaced Pérez Jiménez. The naval branch of the military seemed to have more liberal figures than the army. The year-long Larrazábal regime, from 1958 to 1959, brought back the liberals, the exiles, and Acción Democrática. Larrazábal, a candidate for the presidency in the elections of 1963, was undoubtedly a liberal himself. He also demonstrated a good grasp of the forces which have been agitating Venezuela. He raised the royalty and tax upon the oil industry from 50 per cent to 60 per cent.

During this period it also appeared that the masses, organized labor, the students, the Left, and the left-of-center Acción Democrática were more radical, restless, and subject to political fever than Larrazábal suspected. The violence shown during the Venezuelan visit of Vice-President Richard Nixon of the United States was a sign of the unrest and of the resurgence of Communism and Communist expectations. The name of the Communist chieftain, Gustavo Machado, reappeared thirty years after his first suppression by Gómez. In spite of all these signs, Larrazábal's civic sense won over his military training and he allowed presidential elections to take place that year, as scheduled. The elections of December 1958 led to Larrazábal's defeat, even thought he headed the government. Rómulo Betancourt was elected president, and took office early in 1959.

Betancourt's return to high office, a return which has endured for its full term, gave new and sometimes violent energy to Venezuelan politics. A new and invigorated Communist Party, mixed with and sometimes confused with the Castroism from Cuba, agitated the Betancourt era. Attempted assassinations, rightist plots, and workers' and students' strikes were very frequent. Betancourt himself was the personal target of both Trujillo of the Dominican Republic and Castro of Cuba, who carried on propaganda against him. He made many enemies at home, including the Communist Party. Party leaders of other groups in Venezuela, who controlled Congress, broke with Acción Democrática, as well as with Betancourt. A popular national leader and a strong president, Betancourt was nevertheless a minority president who had no majority in the congress. Only blocs and coalitions made possible the passage of laws he wanted.[4]

Betancourt and his Acción Democrática program did well during his four-year term. Constitutional changes had shortened the president's term and renewed the ban against any man being elected to two successive terms. The elections set for December 1963 returned to the limelight the generation which had shared Venezuela's growing liberalism with Betancourt. An entire group of men, who appeared first in 1928 and again in 1935, have become his political rivals: Jóvito Villalba, of the Democratic Republican Union; Rafael Calders, of the fairly new Christian-Catholic party (COPEI); and the liberal Navy officer, Admiral Wolfgang Larrazábal, who again sought to satisfy his ambition to be president as the candidate of the Popular Democratic Force. Instead of Rómulo Gallegos, twice temporary president, the Acción Democrática nominated for president Raúl Leoni. Leoni, a member of the revolutionary junta of 1945, is an important career politician as well as an intellectual.

In spite of the generally normal political behavior among the leading parties and candidates, a great many Communist and terrorist incidents have occurred since 1960. Beginning with the attempt on the life of Betancourt, violence moved into public and almost-criminal acts of sabotage and destruction. An organization calling itself the FALN (Armed Forces for National Liberation), blessed by Gustavo Machado (the Communist leader and member of congress) and

[4] Betancourt explained his program in his pamphlet *Venezuela Rinde Cuentas* (Costa Rica, 1962); the Inter-American Association for Democracy and Freedom put out a booklet in 1963 on "Rómulo Betancourt: President of Venezuela. A Tribute on his Visit to the United States, February 19-23, 1963."

Fidel Castro of Cuba, claimed that it was acting in the name of national liberation. It appeared to be a coalition of Communist and leftist groups, probably breaking out just in time to weaken government order and suspend the elections. It might have paved the way for either an overthrow or a dictatorship, either a military or a workers' coup d'état. A military coup probably would be more in line with Venezuelan history and experience, while any Communist-led attempt would reveal the new radicalization of Venezuela and the influence of Cuba and even perhaps of nearby British Guiana.

Acción Democrática did not succeed, during Betancourt's term, in matching the working-class unity of the Left with any unity among the social liberals. No permanent coalition brought agreement among the liberal parties. Acción Democrática and COPEI are quite far apart. Jóvito Villalba, who has expressed neutrality towards Fidel Castro's Cuba, broke with Gustavo Machado and the Communists only two months before the elections. The Communist Party, never acceptable to Betancourt, was suspended. The MIR (Movimiento Independiente Revolucionario), another close-to-Communism front, was also barred from the 1963 elections. In spite of these actions, and the guerrilla-like terrorism of the FALN, there is as yet no plan to make the Communist Party illegal. Individual Communists, however, have been penalized. Venezuela's congress (for political reasons) and Venezuela's supreme court (for judicial reasons) have evaded outlawing the Communist Party. Communism in Venezuela is only boycotted.

The over eight million Venezuelans ignored the FALN and its destructive acts and squarely faced the civic but confusing alternatives of choosing from among several almost equally liberal candidates. Betancourt did as much as he could to make the first civilian elections a success, but took many police and military precautions in the interior and along the coast. Because of his opposition in congress, and his minority political role, he had been forced back upon his power over Acción Democrática and his popularity, based upon his social and educational reforms and his protection of big business. Battles against Betancourt in congress have been as severe as those at the polls or in newspaper editorials.

The last few years have brought into politics and the economy a great many new rich. Urban life, an expanded middle class, and an assertive working class have challenged the intellectuals as the one-time elite of the country. Representative democracy, political parties, and socializing programs are a sign of the revolt of the masses as well as of the rise of the middle class. Within the larger Latin American heritage of humanists, classicists, churchmen, and philosophers, the social-thinking Venezuelan is a new figure. But power and economic strength are still concentrated in Caracas, even though a vast natural wealth is to be found in the western, southern, and eastern provinces. It remains to be seen whether the new order of Betancourt and Acción Democrática will go forth from Caracas to the masses of country people, oil and mineral workers, and others who are far from the capital of elite and power structure in Venezuela.

A big-business society, but with a more equitable distribution of land and a more firmly established system of trade unions, was being forged in Venezuela with chances of better success than the previous political society. Politics were still personal, and with a strong feudal flavor. Business was modern, technological, and incorporated. The government's long- and well-established Corporación de Fomento, or Venezuelan Development Corporation, was already fifteen years old in 1963; it was older and more stable than almost all of the parties. The corporation was the chief government channel for all the private capital coming into Venezuela; it was also the government's money-lender to big industry and big business. In the Andes, the Caribbean, or the Orinoco, the vast riches of the Venezuelan subsoil made it possible for the corporation to provide energy, profits, and benefits to the new rich and the emerging businessman's society. The government's most recent step was to create a Four-Year Plan (1963-66) designed to promote private as well as public confidence in industrialization.

Part of this was done to make the government less dependent upon oil—although the higher oil royalties, in turn, made it possible for the government to undertake all this. Oil revenues not only helped agrarian and social reforms; it also made industrial and other public development possible. The industrial revolution of present-day Venezuela identified and associated the government with some of the biggest business in today's world, especially in the exploitation of oil, aluminum, nickel, manganese, iron ore, and other resources. One result has been the regional and even commodity subdivision of the Venezuelan Development Corporation. A branch of the corporation has been set up in the old royalist province of Guayana, now the state of Bolívar, the geographical heart of the new industrialization, while a special subdivision has been created to develop electrical power. Oil, industry, and electric power are the cornerstones of the new Venezuela.[5]

The old real estate, ranching, commercial, and hotel-tourist forces of Venezuela, economically and socially established at Caracas, but politically derived from Andean Táchira, have watched a transformation of the Venezuelan economy. This recent transformation does not, and cannot, do without its oil and landed aristocracy. To these have been added the new millionaires, executives, managers, lawyers, engineers, and technological experts. The historical "Establishment" in Venezuela, located and almost fixed in Caracas but physically invaded and controlled by "outside" caudillo-politicians from time to time, is now seeing the emergence of another class. Economic and social modernization, together with the rise of a monied working class, are finding expression in society and in political life. Almost all parties have begun to think along these lines. Venezuelan values, like the Venezuelan economy and society, have received from the present government the impulse to look for progress in education, housing, small ownership, as well as social security.

Elections, 1963, and the New President, 1964

The elections of December 1963[6] were for the selection of a house of deputies, a senate, state legislatures and municipal councils, and a president. The results showed that Raúl Leoni was elected president by an unusually heavy turnout of voters. The size of the popular vote indicated the strong civilian and electoral faith that had been built up in the country.

The success of the Social Christian candidate, Rafael Caldera, was heralded by a large vote, signifying the emergence of that party to national prominence. Christian social and political circles hailed the vote for COPEI as reaching even further down among the masses than the victory of Acción Democrática. The government party did not carry off the congressional elections; thus the legislative blocs and

[5] No single economic geography is as yet available on the raw materials growth of Venezuela and the new industry.

[6] The New York Times, December 1-3, 1963.

coalitions which marked the Betancourt presidency will probably continue to be necessary.

Raúl Leoni was expected to take over his office in March, 1964. He cut a much less radical and doctrinaire figure than Betancourt. Leoni, more of a political and organization man, was from the state of Bolívar in eastern Venezuela. Born in 1905, he was one of the student leaders of the University of Caracas movement in 1928. He is therefore an old-timer in the circles of Acción Democrática, with critics inside and out who fail to perceive any intellectual spark in him and who are irritated by politics, patronage, and slow motion. Viewed, together with his party, as a radical by the upper classes and as a rightist by the students, Leoni seemed to be more of a middle-of-the-road and moderate liberal. Some reporters expected him to slow down the extreme legislation and to blur the socialist image of the Acción Democrática in order to win the support of big property, Caracas society, and the people of town and country.

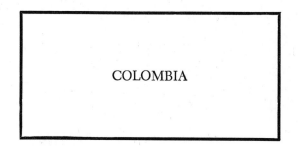

COLOMBIA

ONE

COLOMBIA TODAY

The Violencia

The two chief political forces in Colombia today are— as they have been for the past one hundred years—conservatism and liberalism. The recently negotiated harmony between these two forces has brought to Colombia a degree of political stability which—though tenuous, perhaps—may well be unique in Latin America.

Nevertheless, the country continues to be torn by what Colombians refer to as the *violencia*—a series of violent incidents perpetrated in the mountainous areas, along country roads, and in the city slums. The bandits have no apparent political motivation, and their work resembles that of nineteenth-century highwaymen more than that of twentieth-century revolutionaries.[1]

The *violencia* (which thus far is estimated to have cost the lives of 200,000 Colombians) began in 1948, after the assassination of the liberal, left-of-center presidential candidate, Jorge Eliecer Gaitán in Bogotá. The bloody riots precipitated by that event developed into a state of near-anarchy which has endured ever since. The outbreaks did aggravate old geographic and political rivalries and provoke deep political suspicion, but to this day it is difficult to define the nature of the struggle. It was mutiny, perhaps, that broke out against the con-

[1] Harry Bernstein, *Modern and Contemporary Latin America* (Chicago, 1952), Part V; "Colombia," pp. 573-672; John D. Martz, *Colombia: A Contemporary Political Survey* (Chapel Hill, 1962), pp. 327-36.

servative government then in power; banditry, rather than subversion, that raged against the army and the police.[2]

However unclear the causes of the disorders, their effect was plain enough: the abrupt end of civilian government in Colombia. In 1953, the army forced out President Laureano Gómez, prototype of Colombian conservatism, dissolved the constitutional government, and installed strong-man General Gustavo Rojas Pinilla.

During his five-year rule (1953-57), Rojas Pinilla did a great deal to localize the disturbances, but he proposed no social changes or agrarian reforms that might have done away with their causes; he introduced no political improvements that might have assuaged the popular unrest. Furthermore, his repressive measures had far more of an effect on urban liberals and professionals than on the mountain bandits. His censorship of the press, for instance, did nothing to hamper the illiterate outlaws, but it deprived the cultured classes of an essential liberty.

The Pact of 1957

The Pinilla dictatorship toppled in 1957, when the conservatives and the liberals decided to put an end to their century-old feud (and, hopefully, to the internal disorder) by a written political agreement. Initiated and signed by the conservative ex-President Laureano Gómez and the liberal former Acting President Alberto Lleras Camargo, the pact was designed to last for sixteen years, or until 1974. (A national plebiscite endorsed the arrangements agreed upon by the party leaders, although factions in both parties expressed opposition.) The outstanding feature of the pact was that it provided for each of the two major parties to hold presidential office for alternate four-year terms. The pact also distributed between the two parties offices in the cabinet, the congress, and the local (provincial) councils. (Department legislative seats were also to become part of this distribution agreement.) In an attempt to hasten and assure political democracy, the pact established a civil service system. This provision, it was hoped, would assure stability, encourage the development of electoral

[2] For an analysis of these events see Vernon Fluharty, *Dance of the Millions: Military Rule and the Social Revolution in Colombia, 1930-1956* (Pittsburgh, 1957); see also W. O. Galbraith, *Colombia: A General Survey* (London, 1953).

democracy, and deepen the historic experience with law and order.

A new constitution restored civil government, a judiciary, and free elections. But the 1957 agreement was, in a way, supraconstitutional. Thoroughly practical in nature and not based on any formal political theory or philosophy, it served to widen the gulf between Colombia and the current political trend in Latin America.

The first president under the new coalition was the liberal Alberto Lleras Camargo. His term (1958-62) provided a breathing spell in which to determine the best means of effecting moderate social change.

As the political parties evolved a measure of stability, the social critics, literary radicals, and revolutionary planners who still hold sway in much of Latin America was replaced in Colombia by political moderates, newspaper publishers and editors, university officials, businessmen, and Church leaders—all of whom have exerted their influence to help calm the political storms of the past. Even the military has withdrawn to barracks. The cotton textile manufacturers of Medellín, the oilmen of the Caribbean, the coffee-growers of Bucaramanga, the bankers of Bogotá—all are concerned about the protection of property and profit through the maintenance of law and order. Trade unions have been legalized. Although the demand for agrarian reform increases, dominant business groups and political leaders insist that the need for industrialization is more urgent. They hold that business development, full employment, and a diversified economy are necessary to finance agrarian reforms and to stabilize industrial labor gains.

The newspapers, both liberal and conservative, have contributed heavily to the view that social evolution, not revolution, should be Colombia's road to the future. The liberal view is expressed through *El Tiempo*; the conservative, through *El Siglo*. (The editors and owners of both papers have held high government offices.) Both agree that the main goals for Colombia today are law and order, stability, personal liberty, and elected civilian government.

The Church (which the constitution of 1957 made an official part of the State) continues to wield a strong influence. Colombia has also entered into a concordat with the Vatican. Within the Church, the very intellectual and influential Society of Jesus is an effective pillar of conservatism, but neither liberals nor conservatives have recently attacked the church. Liberals, however, do not support all the positions of the Church, especially in matters of education.

The Educational System

Perhaps the most pressing need in Colombia today is that for a reform of the educational system. Forty-two per cent of the population of fourteen million is illiterate; only 50-60 per cent of the children attend school—and a great many of these go part-time, and then only in certain seasons. Secondary education is inadequate; vocational and technical courses are woefully weak. The teachers are few and poorly trained. This not only affects classroom teaching, but also obviates teachers as molders of public opinion. Thus, except in the large cities, public opinion is formed by local journals, pulpit exhortations, and neighborly gossip.

Although the ministry of education occupies the highest rung on the administrative ladder, its ambitious programs for educational reform find a major obstacle in the apathy of the lower classes.

Surprisingly enough, important improvements have been made in higher education. Colombian universities are neither old nor traditional, as are those of Mexico, Peru, Chile, and Argentina. The Universidad Nacional (National University) at Bogotá is the largest in Colombia. Located in the nation's capital, the National University has a leading role in many affairs; its students are too near the heart of national politics to be ignorant of current growth patterns. But the educational standards of the University are not high; the faculty is all part-time, and underpaid. The University is heavily subsidized by the Ministry of Education, yet intellectually qualified students are frequently unable to matriculate because tuition is too costly for them. Of those who can matriculate, few remain to graduate. Many go abroad to study—in contrast to demands made on his pocketbook, little demand is made on the student's time and intelligence for a degree. The great University Reform of 1918 which swept Latin America had little influence in Colombia, but a reform movement more concerned than that of 1918 with the development of scholarly and scientific faculties is currently afoot there. Until recently, Colombian universities, like others in Latin America, were groupings of professional schools drawing their students directly from among the *colegios* (the secondary schools) and training from them a professional elite without benefit of an undergraduate curriculum in the liberal arts. The introduction of liberal arts faculties in schools of arts and sciences is a recent innovation. The introduction of these faculties of philosophy and letters, as they are called, has been opposed by many students, as well as faculty and administrators of a conservative cast. But it is clear that only such innovations can raise the quality of university graduates.

The Universidad de los Andes, privately organized and very new, quickly became famous throughout the Hemisphere. It has been particularly encouraged and guided by ex-President Alberto Lleras Camargo, its leading spirit and first rector. The University of the Andes has strong friends and influential alumni in spite of its small size and recent establishment. Viewed as a model for other Colombian universities, Los Andes maintains interuniversity relations with one or two of them. Time will prove its impact upon society, business, and government.

Another major influence upon Colombia's present and future is in the southern region. The Universidad del Valle (University of The Valley) is in the city of Cali, at the upper end of the Cauca River valley. Less than twenty years old, the university is one of the newer lights of Latin America. The medical school and library are already famous in the United States and Latin America. El Valle has also been concerned with the social sciences and the humanities. The University promises, through its ten-year development plan, to become a major university. Located in the heart of a wealthy and expanding region, the Universidad del Valle, like the city of Cali itself, represents twentieth-century Colombia. Although surrounded by social and ecclesiastical conservatism, Cali moves in response to technical, capitalist, scientific, and business motives.

Socio-Economic Problems

Far more than with educational reform, the masses of Colombians are concerned with the socio-economic problems which beset the nation. One of them—inflation—is very critical. The consequences of the upward spiral of prices and rents in the 1952-63 period have been felt by all the classes and all the segments of the society.

The current emphasis on diversification of industry is an attempt to offset the traditional fluctuations of a one-commodity (coffee) economy. The emphasis is all the stronger because other remedies typical of Latin America cannot be applied in Colombia. For instance, the land expropriation and redistribution programs so popular in many Latin American countries are effective only when the land is divided into a relatively few large estates. In Colombia, however, two thirds of the coffee produced is grown by individual families on their own plots of less than ten acres.

This widespread ownership of rural lands may help to explain certain aspects of the Colombian scene. Much of the unrest which prevails throughout the rural areas, as well as the apathy toward educational reform, may be attributed to the fall in the international price of coffee in recent years. Also, the farmer who owns his own land, or who has a long lease on the land he rents, has an understandable lack of interest in the urban drive toward industrialization, and to agrarian radicalism as well. To be sure, the peasant wants land, but he wants it on an individual, not a collective basis. Finally, the farmer who owns his land resents the need, however pressing, to look for work in the city.[3] His natural reluctance is increased by the fact that industrial development has not yet been rapid enough to absorb the rural influx or to offset the losses in coffee revenues. Indeed, industrialization, even on the limited scale on which it has proceeded, has only the excess of imports over exports and the shortage of dollars.

During Camargo's term in office, an austerity program was introduced and government spending reduced. Instead of resorting to the five- or six-year plans typical of other Latin American countries, Camargo created a National Planning Council and staffed it with technicians and engineers who, with considerable financial aid from the United States, avoided grandiose schemes in favor of gradual, step-by-step modernization of industrial and technical sectors of the national economy.

These measures have met with a certain amount of success. By 1962, when León Valencia became president, although the Colombian peso had been devalued, the economic picture looked brighter:

[3] Orlando Fals-Borda, *Peasant Society in the Colombian Andes: A Sociological Study of Saucío* (Gainesville, 1935); Gerardo and Alicia Reichel Dalmatoff, *The People of Aritama: The Cultural Personality of a Colombian Mestizo Village* (Chicago, 1961).

coffee revenues had increased, land reforms (limited chiefly to public lands) had been introduced, most of the labor force was employed, and national attention was drawn to the development of the country's mineral wealth, and the construction of railways and highways, particularly in the underpopulated border regions.

It is as yet too early to evaluate the performance of the Valencia administration. In 1963, the economic and political balance which had endured since 1957 seemed to be suffering new strains: inflation had again become a serious problem; the sporadic outbreaks of violence had spread from rural areas to the cities.

But, thus far at least, Colombia has managed to avoid the political extremism found in some of her nearest neighbors. The Communist Party reached its high point in the 1940's; since then, it has steadily declined in influence and power. The disturbances which continue to occur are less the result of any international conspiracy than purely local reactions to domestic social, economic, and educational problems. As such, they are an inevitable part of the Colombian historic experience.

Colombia has still a great deal to do, but her concern for political stability is great. For the government and the people realize that only in the presence of law and order can the desired progress and modernization take place.

TWO

The Indians

The Indians who lived in Colombia before 1500 ranged in cultural level from the coastal peoples and the forest fishing and hunting peoples up to the Chibcha society of the Andes. The Chibcha society of Colombia was in some ways as advanced as the better-known Indian cultures of Mexico and Peru. The Chibcha stand out culturally above the numerous Indian communities along the Caribbean, the Cauca and Magdalena River valleys, and the upper Amazon. The Chibcha, of course, also stand out geographically, located as they were in the high plateau where the present-day capital of Bogotá is.

The Colombian Chibcha had mastered the mining of gold and the cultivation of corn and potatoes—products which were to tie them to the Europeans. They were at the center of a wide gold and agricultural-using zone which extended into Panama and Central America, Ecuador and Peru, and eastward into Venezuela. Nevertheless, although their language, legends, agricultural knowledge, and artistic use of gold brought them to an advanced cultural level, they never attained either the urban development or the political organization of the Aztecs, the Mayas, or the Incas. The Chibcha left few great architectural monuments. There are no remains of cities, great buildings, or roadways. No record exists to prove the presence of any codices (pictograph manuscripts), stelae (stone monuments with carved writing and numbers), colored mural paintings, or temple carvings. They lacked the artistic, architectural, and structural-engineering accomplishments of their famous neighbors.

Chibcha artistry and craftsmanship in the working of gold was excellent. But it was also their ruin. The Spanish believed in the legend of El Dorado, true or not. The fabled man of gold was the metallic magnet which attracted the conquerors. Colombians themselves made their fortunes in later centuries by raiding the graves of Chibcha chiefs and nobles, which were filled with jewelry and objects of gold. Robbing these tombs (*huacas*), a busy and profitable occupation know as *huaquería*, was as usual in Colombia as it was in Egypt. This subterranean search for gold was widely carried on into the nineteenth century and even into the twentieth. It must be put alongside the more technological and capitalistic mining operations of modern times as one of the historic sources of Colombian riches.

The Indians were also farmers. Chibcha and non-Chibcha alike knew how to produce potatoes, beans, and maize. The farming Indian society extended up along the two great river valleys of the Cauca and Magdalena, as well as through the mountain and plateau districts. The available archaeological and historical knowledge of early Colombian peoples is probably more meager than that of any primitive society in America. It is clear, however, that they were politically divided into tribes living in about twenty large provinces. The twenty tribes (the Chibcha were only one of these) adapted their lives to the different natural aspects of the provinces they inhabited. There were coastal, river, plateau, and mountain Indian societies.[1]

The Coming of the White Men

The Europeans pushed into this little-known and varied cultural area from three different directions, each invasion arriving before 1550. One wing established footholds along the Caribbean at two points. Then it moved into the interior by way of the Cauca and

---

[1] *Handbook of the South American Indian,* Bulletin Number 143 (Washington, D.C.: Smithsonian Institution, Bureau of Ethnology), 1946-1950, Vol. II: "Andean Civilizations," pp. 50-55, 823-979; Vol. V: "The Circum-Caribbean Tribes," pp. 11-20, 297-402. Gregorio Hernández de Alba is the leading Colombian student of the Indian; Indianist work is carried on at the Institute of Andean Research, Bogotá.

Magdalena valleys. Another group of conquerors, this time German, came across the Andes from Venezuela to Bogotá. (The Caribbean, therefore, was the earliest route of Colombian discovery and colonial settlement.) The third group, Spaniards fresh from the conquest of Peru, had ventured north from Peru into Ecuador. They went on to reach Bogotá by following the high Andean trails.

In a celebrated and dramatic meeting in 1538, the three bands of Europeans came together at the Chibcha settlement, on the cold plain near Bogotá. (Pedro de Cieza de León, a young eyewitness and participant, described the early Indian-Spanish encounters in his famous *Chronicle of Peru*.) The Spanish lawyer, Gonzalo Jiménez de Quesada, succeeded in establishing his leadership as the discoverer and conqueror of Bogotá and the Chibcha. The Germans returned to Venezuela. The conquistadors who had come up from Peru went back to newly founded Cali, using that southern site as a base for further exploring expeditions to the Pacific Coast and inland along the river valleys.[2]

Jorge Robledo was one of the greatest explorers of inland Colombia. He moved north from Cali to the famous and rich valley of Antioquía which was discovered in 1546. Antioquía's most important city, Medellín, was founded a century later. While Bogotá was becoming an administrative and political center of New Granada, other regions were also being settled. Antioquía was the main mining region; Cartagena and Santa Marta, along the Caribbean, were the sites of both agricultural and commercial operations. Indians were the labor force of the mountains. Negro slaves brought from Africa predominated along the coast.

Royal government followed quickly. Wealthy proprietors and rival claimants to territory and rule soon lost their power to royal governors, judges, and officials. The *audiencia* (supreme court) established at Bogotá in 1549 remained the chief instrument of royal authority in New Granada until the Crown created the Viceroyalty of New Granada in 1717. The Catholic Church also set up religious dioceses and monastic provinces. The city council, the *cabildo*, took care of the limited municipal and town functions. The active and adventuresome years were over by 1550.

[2] The only single-volume general history in English is J. M. Henao and G. Arrubla, *History of Colombia*, translated by J. Fred Rippy (Chapel Hill, 1938).

White, Spanish immigrants arrived steadily. The Indian population declined. The African Negro population increased in spite of the rigors of slavery. The *encomienda* system of forced Indian labor existed alongside the plantation system which exploited Negro slave labor. Both slavery and *encomienda* also provided the work force of Indians and Negroes for the gold mines. Disease and alcoholism helped wear down the natives long before the gold veins were exhausted. Race mixtures among Spaniards, Indians and Negroes also reduced the pure strains of Amerindian and African, replacing them with *mestizo* and colored peoples.

Agriculture, especially the plantation system near the coast, supported an aristocracy which kept away from such intermarriage. Race and caste followed class and property lines. Tradition, conservatism, Spanishness, and pride of position helped keep a white strain intact in Colombia. Contact and connection with high Church and government offices provided this upper class with political power as well as with social leadership. Descendants of the early conquerors, as well as fortunate and influential newcomers, acquired large land grants and high social status. Colombia's colonial aristocracy tried to imitate the Spanish aristocracy, although there were no grandees and not every wealthy creole held a title of nobility.

By 1600 the process of Hispanicizing the colony called Santa Fé de Bogotá or Santa Fé was well underway. Spanish policy toward the Indians became increasingly paternal and protective, seeking both to break down the *encomienda* system and to build up royal and ecclesiastical control. Many white colonists of Spanish origin were neither nobles nor privileged, but had some wealth or income. These "commoner" men of commercial, military, or even factory interests were free in status, and owned rural or urban property. They might well be called a "middle class," socially and politically. Many of them were creole—that is, born in the colony; others had come over from Spain. They also enjoyed the personal services and labor of Indians. This provided them with an economic vested interest in the colonial system and its institutions.

Nevertheless the Crown, through the *audiencia*, had its own ideas about society, government, and Indian labor. Some valuable reports, histories, and memorials provide the materials for our information about those days. In 1614 the *audiencia* sent Judge Francisco Herrera y Campuzano to make an investigation of conditions and report on them. The Campuzano manuscripts now in Bogotá are a documentary gold mine on Indian-white race and economic relations in seventeenth century Colombia. Judge Campuzano recommended that the Indians be separated from the white and Negroes and placed in reservations and villages under their own *caciques* or chiefs. This segregation was designed for the Indians' own protection, but it did not succeed in depriving the whites of Indian labor, nor did it end the mixture of races.

The Negroes

The original concentration of Negro slavery along the Caribbean changed with time. Negroes were brought up into the mountain mining districts. Caste, class, and color continued to be related and the Colombian Negro remained among the low social orders. For the most part, however, the Negroes stayed along the Pacific and the Caribbean coasts. Bound up with plantation society more than with ranching or mining, the Negroes along the northern coast were socially and culturally akin to their fellow-Africans in other Caribbean lands.[3]

Many African tribes were represented among the Negro groupings. In Venezuela, there were almost as many variations within the Negro society itself as among the Indians. Race mixtures helped to erase the different cultural traits of white and Negro or within the Negro groups. The colored or mulatto peoples were also mainly settled along the coasts, and in the cities and towns rather than in the countryside. Like the *mestizo* of Indian-white origin, the mulatto of Negro-white origin also aspired to higher social and economic status. Rarely, however, did the *mestizo* or mulatto reach positions of political power and influence beyond the town and village level. City and colonial government positions were reserved for white creoles and Spaniards.

The creole and the Spaniard constituted the two social strata of the upper class which dominated colonial society. The creole whites, often wealthy, were the local leaders of town and rural society. The European-born whites monopolized the important institutions of co-

[3] Only a few books have ever been written about the Negro in Colombia.

lonial power: the Church, the *audiencia*, the army, trade, and the capital. The Europeans served Spain's centralizing and imperial needs for an overseas ruling class. Because the Spaniards often went back to Spain after a time, they rarely put down roots in colonial Colombia. The creole stayed on the scene and became the leader of local, regional-sectional, and prenational interests.

Government and Institutions

Spanish government and institutions in Colombia did not change much before 1700. From 1550 to 1700, when English and European piracy and wars flung raiders and invaders at Panama, Cartagena, and other points of the colony, the Spanish home government tightened colonial defenses but did not alter the governmental structure.

Aggressors assaulted Cartagena; privateers and buccaneers expected to seize rich prizes from the great trans-Atlantic and trans-Caribbean fleets that sailed the Spanish Main. These fleets carried goods from Europe to the New World. Bringing back gold, silver, and valued raw materials from the Indies to Europe, the fleets used Cartagena as a major rendezvous and point of deposit. This was the famed *tierra firme* fleet, different from another one which went to Veracruz, Mexico. A permanent Caribbean naval station, known as the Windward Fleet, was supported by special taxes levied upon Colombian and Venezuelan colonists. The great Porto Bello fair, held in what is now Panama, was a famous marketplace for vast commercial activity. Porto Bello lived for that animating fair; the town died when the annual fair was over and was revived only when the fair was renewed the next year. But Porto Bello never really was able to rival Cartagena or Panama within the Colombian colony.

Mining, especially of emeralds and gold, was another source of wealth. New Granada was the greatest producer of gold in all the Indies. In addition to their mining and foreign trade, New Granadans also cultivated tobacco. Tobacco was not grown on big estates or plantations and did not therefore require slave labor. Tobacco farms were readily worked by individual owners and their large families (just as much coffee is raised today). Owned and cultivated for the most part by creole commoners and *mestizo* peasants, tobacco was another important product of the colony in the eighteenth century.

During most of the colonial period, the colony was subject to the administrative domination of the Viceroyalty of Peru in faraway Lima. No rebellion ever loosened the colony's loyalty to the government in remote Madrid or distant Lima. Perhaps the royal judges and administrators in Bogotá were content to be left alone. When changes came to the colony early in the eighteenth century, they were caused by foreign and international factors. The wars of the colonial era finally had their effect. In addition, an increase of contraband trade and smuggling along the Caribbean exposed the weakness of existing Spanish customs and naval systems. The War of the Spanish Succession (1700-14) brought all these hostile elements together in one large onslaught which affected Spain and its ruling dynasty. Only then were changes ordered from Madrid. The first quarter of the eighteenth century reshaped the political command at Bogotá—the first major government reorganization since 1549.

THREE

VICEROYALTY INTO NATION

The Viceroyalty of New Granada

The Viceroyalty of New Granada was created in 1717. Its jurisdiction included present-day Colombia, Panama, Ecuador, and Venezuela. But this territorial reorganization was so closely bound up with Caribbean commerce, the slave trade, and defense, that it did not last long. Madrid had to give more self-government to Venezuela. After 1742, the captain-general and governor of Caracas no longer answered to Bogotá. The vast territory of New Granada fronted upon two oceans and provided a barrier for the protection of the wealth of Peru and access to the Pacific. Pressure to discontinue the Viceroyalty led to its temporary abolition in 1724. But the Viceroyalty was restored in 1740 and remained effective until 1810, when the War for Independence brought changes.

The succession of viceroys who administered this varied and extensive "new kingdom" of New Granada left a strong impress upon the last century of colonial life. Their names and deeds need not detain us here. After 1750, the pressing need for funds to defend the colony coincided with the appearance of a spirit of reform and improvement in Spain. This spirit brought changes and reforms in New Granada. As time went on, each of the viceroys took up one or more matters of government, sometimes in a dull and routine fashion, sometimes in a capable and efficient way. Almost all the viceroys had something to propose or enact with respect to factories, roads, the royal mint, taxation, or even natural disasters such as earthquakes and the shocking destruction left in their wake. One of the most important and historic events was the expulsion of the Jesuits in 1767. The Jesuit missions on the remote frontiers of the Mota and Orinoco Rivers, as well as their well-endowed colleges and properties in Quito, Bogotá, Popayán, Antioquia, Tunja, and elsewhere were taken over by the viceroy in the name of the Crown.

The viceroyalty of Manuel de Guirior (1773-76) coincided even more closely with the changes going on in Spain and Latin America. New Granada, like the other colonies, could take its own steps toward the improvement of education and internal and foreign trade. Ten years earlier, the famous astronomer-naturalist, José Celestino Mutis, had come from Spain to work and teach in Bogotá. Viceroy Guirior recommended steps for the improvement of education and the arts. He suggested to Madrid that a university be established so that the youth of New Granada might be as well instructed as those in Mexico City, Cordoba (Argentina), or Lima. Guirior was one of the earliest viceroys to confront some of those Church-State relations which were to give modern Colombia one of her bitterest issues. He enforced the anti-Jesuit decree and then left New Granada to go on to his new post as viceroy of Peru.

Revolt of the Communes

The reign of Guirior's successor was marked by the tumultuous sedition popularly known as the *comunero* revolt.[1] The revolt of the communes in 1780 in Colombia coincided with the famous Indian uprising of the Tupac Amaru in Peru and Bolivia. The Andes seethed with unrest. In fact, for the next generation—down to the eve of Independence—New Granada was charged with sparks of revolution, enlightenment, and unrest. The New Granada commune uprising of 1780 was a movement which appeared chiefly in the northern parts of

[1] J. M. Henoa and G. Arrubla, *History of Colombia*, translated by J. Fred Rippy (Chapel Hill, 1938), pp. 274-75; Harry Bernstein, *Modern and Contemporary Latin America* (Chicago: 1952), pp. 580-84.

the colony. Its leaders opposed the colonial sales tax, the tax to support the Windward Fleet, and the head or poll tax. The movement was antitax, but not anti-Spain; it did not seek revolution, only reform. The famous thirty-six articles of the *comunero* leaders represent the creole and tobacco farmers' complaints against Spanish rule in New Granada.

Reformers and Radicals

Accompanying the *comunero* revolt, as a sort of revolt within a revolt, was the Indian rebellion against the "theft" of Indian clan and tribal lands (which was mentioned in the thirty-six articles). The force of the revolt carried the rebels into Bogotá and brought about the surrender of the royal authorities. Soon, however, the government retracted its surrender. One famous *comunero*, José Antonio Galán, held out until he was caught and executed in 1782. Although he lost his life, he became one of the earliest patriots of modern Colombia. The revolt of the *comuneros* represents a petition against wrongs done to the people in the last years of the colonial period.

The unrest was also caused by the creole state of mind that was emerging at the end of the colonial era. Even the viceroys had favored improvements in education, science, and learning. Several of them repeatedly supported the establishment of a public university. In 1791 Colombia's first newspaper, the *Papel Periódico*, appeared. This weekly was able to make use of a local printing press.

There was in Bogotá a young man of twenty-nine, Antonio Nariño, who brought the ideas of the French Revolution to New Granada. Born of a wealthy creole family, he was also lucky enough to hold a high government position. His home in Bogotá was a salon for other creoles of his generation: Francisco de Caldas, Camilo Torres, Jorge Tadeo Lozano. Nariño was a link between the reformist aspiration of the *comunero* movement and the new optimism connected with the revolutionary era and independence. Nariño became the senior figure of Colombian nationalism: he was not only a precursor of independence but also the successful patriot who helped to bring it about. His first claim to fame was his translation into Spanish of the French Declaration of the Rights of Man, which he published in Bogotá. Sedition and Jacobinism had already entered the colony. The alarmed viceroy arrested and exiled Nariño, who escaped. Between 1797 and 1803 he was one of the boldest and most persevering creole patriots in northern South America.[2]

Colombia in 1800 had also a great reputation for intellectual and scientific activity. There were theaters and clubs, as well as newspapers and political radicalism. These progressive ideas arose in part from the study of science in an Age of Reason. Scientists drew the attention and praise of Alexander von Humboldt and Aimé Bonpland, the noted European savants who visited and stayed in New Granada early in the nineteenth century. Distinguished colonial figures such as Felix Restrepo and Francisco de Caldas, together with the naturalist José Mutis, gave true scientific character to New Granada.

Beneath this level of scientific progress and political thinking among the creoles lay the hard and inert floor of the masses. There were about two million people in the colony; among most of them little progress was made and no spirit of inquiry existed. Things changed little from one generation to another. The condition of the Indians and Negroes in colonial New Granada was much the same as in other parts of America. Beggary was widespread and idleness was a constant source of official complaint. The lower classes were rich only in alcoholism and apathy. The *comunero* revolt had drawn attention to abject social conditions, but they had hardly changed. Nothing had been done to stop one of the economic reasons for the *comunero* revolt: Spanish acquisition of Indian lands.

One of the later viceroys denounced in 1803 the evil social situation of low wages, beggary, and ignorance which in fact continued past his day and long afterwards:

> Complaint against laziness is general, everyone laments the lack of application to work; but I have not heard of any rise in wages, and I understand that today people pay the same wage as 50 or more years ago, notwithstanding the rise in price of every necessity of life, and therefore the greater profit of agriculture and other *haciendas*, where articles of direct consumption are made or processed. This is an injustice which cannot last long. It seems to me that a day will come in which the laborer will impose the law upon the *hacienda* owners who

[2] For information on Mutis, Nariño, and others, see Bernard Moses, *Spain's Declining Power in South America, 1730-1806* (Berkeley, 1919), pp. 256-91.

will be compelled to have those who took part in producing the gains to share in them.[3]

If this represented in some degree the social or class relations between poor and rich, there still remained as strong as ever the geographic differences among the several provinces. The three great producing regions—Popayán in the south, Cartagena in the north, and Antioquia in the center—were all dominated and directed by Bogotá, the capital, which produced little but administration, law, and authority.

Background of Independence

As the colonial era receded, new events in Spain surged forward in 1808. The gathering Napoleonic storm over Europe startled both New Granadan creoles and Spaniards with its omens of trouble ahead. By August 1808 Bogotá knew that the French had invaded Spain. The last of the Spanish viceroys of New Granada, Antonio Amar y Borbón, had been in Bogotá for five years when these events occurred.

The news of the French invasion in Spain reached Bogotá almost at the same time as the commissioners from the supreme junta at Seville, the chief agency of Spanish resistance to the French. The commissioners wanted to secure an oath of loyalty to the abdicated Spanish monarch, Fernando VII, in whose name the supreme junta was then governing. They also needed revenues—taxes and gold from New Granada. A few months later, in August 1809, a violent reaction broke out at Quito. The rebels protected their actions by declaring for the King of Spain, but they refused to acknowledge the leadership of the supreme junta and instead set up their own supreme junta and did away with the royal *audiencia*.

The Quito junta tried to assert its political leadership over a wide area and offered Popayán (in southern New Granada) and Panama (in northern New Granada) a chance to submit to its jurisdiction. The far-flung challenge to New Granadan autonomy came at a time which compelled a choice and decision: in January 1809 the supreme junta of Seville had raised the Indies colonies of Spain to integral parts of the Spanish monarchy from their former status of royal or Crown colonies. The rebel patriots in Quito thereupon invited the

[3] Bernstein, *op. cit.*, p. 591.

cabildo at Bogotá to send deputies to the Quito junta instead of to the junta in Seville. The changes in Spain and the wide territorial ambitions of the Quito rebels aroused some support for Quito in New Granada. An "American" party rose in sympathy with the Quito rebels, but a "Spanish" party raised its counterpower and influence.

The reaction to this in Bogotá was marked by repression and arrest. Nariño was imprisoned again. There was alarm over the agitation and propaganda supporting the Quito faction. The Bogotá *cabildo* then asked Viceroy Amar y Borbón to call a meeting of the leading citizens and representatives of the corporations and chartered interests in the colony. The viceroy consented, reluctantly but inevitably. He may have known of the consequences of a similar meeting held in the Viceroyalty of Mexico a short time before the Spanish Crown prohibited any such meeting in its .Indies colonies. This first "consultative" body of Colombia met in September 1809, one month after the Quito action.

Camilo Torres, who was to be one of the most vigorous of Colombian creoles in the imminent independence movement, took a prominent part in this assembly. He was the adviser to the Bogotá *cabildo*. Although the assembly itself accomplished nothing, except to reveal the existing divisions between Americans and Spaniards, Torres added to his reputation and following. He defended the cause of the *quiteños* and the rights of all creoles in his celebrated *Memorial of Grievances and Rights* of November 20, 1809. Although not published at that time, because of the opposition of the Spanish party in the Bogotá *cabildo*, Camilo Torres' writings became the cornerstone of Colombian independence. Meantime, while the assembly of 1809 had met and done little, the viceroy's troops had crushed both the revolt and the junta at Quito.

Nevertheless, the spirit of the times penetrated and weakened the victory of the viceroy, the army, the Inquisition, and other authoritative agencies. Because the internal situation in Spain had deteriorated quickly, the Sevilla supreme junta had been replaced by a regency. The regency then decreed the equality of Americans and Spaniards and called for a constitutional convention in Cadiz, Spain, inviting colonial creoles to take part. That convention became famous as one of the sources of Hispanic and Hispanic-American liberalism, reform, and political progress. The pressure of a liberalized Spain thus forced its way into New Granada. It had a curious and unexpected effect there: many conservatives, clericals, "tory" high judges, colonial officials, and favored merchants feared liberalism from the parent country as much, perhaps more, than they opposed it in New Granada: it endangered the very source of their privileges.

No sooner had the viceroy restored Spanish military authority in New Granada than the winds of liberal reform in Spain blew across the Atlantic the news of a constitutional movement in the mother country, asking the support of and proclaiming identity with liberal Colombian creoles. Torres and others were strengthened and invigorated. Strong evidence of a new day was seen in the liberation of Nariño as soon as the Spanish representatives reached New Granada. But the Spanish officials were careful: they gave no sign or hint of encouragement to self-expression in New Granada until an oath of loyalty to the regency for Fernando VII was taken. Although Nariño was freed from prison, he remained under supervision. The Spanish were on guard to prevent any sentiment for freedom or independence.

As long as nonelected bodies such as the *cabildo*, the *audiencia* or the viceroy, which derived their authority from Spain, could maintain their influence, the colonial system and the Spanish institutions would remain intact. They could be reformed, but not overthrown or replaced. But the moment that juntas arose to substitute for and take over such basic political institutions, the Spaniards began to fear the stir of creole demands. They were right: events in 1810 culminated in revolt in July. The *cabildos* of city and town, and the juntas which were their patriotic committees, were the central groups of creole action. These were the revolutionary "cells," although there were also some important leaders who entered the fray at the last minute.

Independence and War

From July to December 1810, the creole movement rolled over New Granada from one end to the other, breaking over the judges of the royal *audiencia* and the viceroy himself. Its force swept Spanish officialdom out of the colony. In July 1810, the Bogotá *cabildo* created its own junta and claimed jurisdiction over New Granada. That was the Colombian revolution.

The Bogotá junta sought supremacy over the whole colony as soon as the hand of Spain was removed. At once there arose from the provinces an enduring regional-sectional resistance to the central government in the capital. The Caribbean city of Cartagena, tied to Spain by heavy commercial investment and mercantile interests, favored the Spanish supreme junta at Seville rather than the junta at Bogotá. Cartagena had large economic and commercial stakes in the Spanish peninsular market and ran the risk of losing her access to the Caribbean markets (Cuba) or her profitable import-export trade with Cadiz and Seville. In fact Cartagena had a stronger vested interest in trade with Cuba and Seville than in trade with Bogotá or interior New Granada. In September 1810, when the Cartagena junta issued a call to all New Granadan regions, small and large, asking for a congress under a federal system, that manifesto was clearly threatening to the Bogotá junta which did not want to be outnumbered and outvoted. But Bogotá had the advantage: it was necessary to centralize New Granada administratively in order to organize to fight the counterattacking royalists.

Under these circumstances it proved possible to get together and hold the "congress" in December 1810. This "congress" took its oath with great ceremony and optimism and tried to get down to work. Camilo Torres was a leading delegate; Antonio Nariño was one of the secretaries. The congress was the legislature, while the Bogotá junta claimed to be the executive. Which was the supreme authority? As a result of conflict between Bogotá and the provinces—that is, between the junta and the congress—delegates began to withdraw. The work of legislation never began. Provincial juntas arose almost everywhere and sectional rivalries became struggles within struggles. Pressure grew for some sort of political first step, and a compromise government emerged.

This first government of Colombia was called *Cundinamarca* (named for the region in which Bogotá lies). A constitution in 1811 made it valid. Although claiming to protect the principle of monarchy, the Cundinamarca government was headed by a president, Jorge Tadeo Lozano. A citizen army was created and an elementary school system was promised. The first constitution of Colombia did not recognize any other religion but Roman Catholicism. Although Lozano was president, the strongest figure in Cundinamarca was Antonio Nariño, who had now risen to important office in the city of Bogotá. In his newspaper, *La Bagatela,* he propagandized those principles of nationalism, unity, and centralism which made him the leading *unitario* figure in New Granada. Opposed to him was the federalist Camilo Torres. These two men represented the first political rivalry within the new government. A short while later, in 1812, Nariño helped overthrow the government, replacing it by one which made him president. He now held the highest position which the Bogotá creoles and government could give him.

Bolívar and Colombia

Meantime, other provinces got together long enough to form their own regional unity in another Congress free from the interference of *bogotanos* and other centralists. Camilo Torres, one of its leaders, was instructed to express sectional interests by forming a states' rights government based upon compacts and a confederation. Established in 1811, the government adopted articles of confederation and took the name of the United Provinces of New Granada. Thus, two governments, Cundinamarca and the United Provinces of New Granada, existed side by side. Soon a third force appeared as Cartagena fell into the hands of patriots who broke with the merchants and issued a declaration of independence from Spain. Shortly afterwards, Simón Bolívar entered Cartagena after his flight from Venezuela and carried his war and revolution from Venezuela into New Granada. The "tories" and pro-Spanish interests along the Caribbean were put down.

Bolívar, who had nothing to do with the liberation of the trading towns along the coast, now developed his strategy of using New Granadan forces to rid the entire viceroyalty of Spanish forces. He then issued his *Memoir to the Citizens of New Granada,* a semi-political document which proposed a united and centralized government in order to win the liberty of both Venezuela and New Granada. The veteran soldiers of both territories would be combined into one army. He had a hard task: Cundinamarca and Nariño held back from any declaration of independence and internal divisions intruded right into the armies, with officers taking one side or the other. Francisco de Paula Santander, at that time a junior officer but later vice-president of New Granada under Bolívar and then president of independent Colombia, was secretary to one officers' movement which resisted Nariño.

Santander wrote:

> The displeasure shown by the towns on account of being deprived of self-government by incorporation with Santa Fé de Bogotá; the protests of the provinces of Pamplona and Casanare; the opposition of the governments of Cartagena and Antioquía against the policies of Bogotá; and above all the energetic note of the government of Caracas led . . . high-ranking officers . . . to refuse to obey Nariño if he insisted on uniting the provinces by force.[4]

In fact Nariño's military campaigns to coerce the provinces were a failure. He was defeated and severely criticized for establishing the separate state of Cundinamarca, with its "dictatorship" centered in Nariño and Bogotá. But he was able to keep his power base in Bogotá and Cundinamarca and once again brought about a compromise with Camilo Torres and the federalists. The new situation, although temporary, gave Bolívar his opportunity.

In 1813, Bolívar was made a citizen of New Granada and a brigadier-general in the army. Encouraged by the enthusiasm of Camilo Torres for the New Granada congress, Bolívar led a combined force of New Granadan and Venezuelan soldiers into the first of a series of reconquests, victories, and triumphs in the Venezuelan *oriente* region, which he reported faithfully to his political superiors in New Granada. But by 1814, his skill and luck had run out. He fled back to New Granada, then to Cartagena, and finally left in 1815 for his famous exile on the island of Jamaica.

There was a taut balance between the New Granada congress and the Nariño government in Cundinamarca. It was the peak of the critical period. Colombians refer to the *patria boba*, the "foolish fatherland" of the years marked by quarrels and an inability to work together. The congress and the executive—or, in other words, Camilo Torres and Antonio Nariño—rarely agreed. The only uplifting note

[4] William M. Gibson, *The Constitutions of Colombia* (Durham, 1948), p. 117

was the decision (chiefly initiated by Nariño) to come out into the open and issue a declaration of independence. So far two regions had issued declarations of independence: Cartagena in 1811 and now Bogotá in 1813.

The worst danger came from the south. Strong Peruvian royalists, seizing Popayán, threatened to move north along the Cauca river valley, menace the wavering loyalty of the important towns and landowners, and then capture the rich mineral centers at Antioquia and the middle river regions. In trying to head off this invasion in 1814, Nariño was defeated and captured by Spanish royalists. Like Francisco de Miranda, the Venezuelan patriot, Nariño was removed from Latin America and taken to the dungeons of Cadiz, Spain. Antioquia was now in grave peril.

Patriots in Colombia

Two great figures took over the defense. One of them was Francisco de Caldas, one of the great scientists of his day and a determined republican patriot. Caldas, a Colombian counterpart of republican-minded scientists in both the French and American Revolutions, had to pay for his ideas with his life. Linked by his scientific interests and republican ideas with the scientific community in the United States, Caldas is one of the outstanding names in Colombian history. In Antioquia, in order to inspire the people, independence was declared. Antioquia organized the defenses of the region and created her first legislature. The legislature adopted the advanced measure of freeing the children of Negro slaves. Thus, before the Spanish reconquest of all Colombia brought the *patria boba* to an end in 1815, several leading states of New Granada had already separately declared their independence from Spain.

The Bogotá government had domestic critics as determined as her royalist-Spanish enemies. Bogotá commanded leading military strength and struggled also to keep the chief sources of revenues and taxation. The local legislatures—that of Antioquia, for example—demanded that these resources be federalized. Independence had awakened not only a sense of nationalism but also the beginnings of federalism. Bogotá and the congress continued at odds in a running debate, congress finally won: it created a junta of three men, one each from Socorro (center of the *comunero* revolt of 1780), Cartagena, and Antioquía. But while Bogotá was defeated by her domestic creole enemies, the use of force again threatened from the outside. At this time Bolívar threw his strength to the side of congress, subdued Bogotá and allowed congress to move the seat of government back there.

But it was too late. Cartagena fell at the end of 1815. The New Granada congress turned executive power over to one man: Camilo Torres. He accepted it as a duty but already felt that the republic was about to expire and that he was not capable of restoring it to life and vigor. He was right. Spain soon took over the country; the congress was dissolved and the deputies fled. Hundreds of people took the road south for their safety. The future president of Colombia, Santander, wrote: "it was only the stern resolution of not dying on the Spanish gallows that gave us strength and perseverance to accomplish the retreat." The five great national figures were also gone: Bolívar, Nariño, Torres, Santander, and Caldas. Caldas and Torres were shot to death by Spanish firing squads.

Pablo Morillo, Generalissimo of the Spanish armies in both Venezuela and Colombia, headed the military government. There were few pardons. Confiscations reduced many to misery and penury. Colombian historians write of the reign of terror which the Spanish restoration brought back. Courts-martial held trials. Women were not exempted from royalist revenge: some female patriots of the Colombian Revolution met a worse fate than the men. After 1816, when General Morillo left to "pacify" Venezuela, a newly appointed Spanish viceroy and *audiencia* came slowly up to Bogotá after waiting in Cartagena. The Jesuits were authorized to return to New Granada, and they, too, re-entered slowly. The old regime turned the clock back—for a short time.

In 1817, Bolívar, moving toward Colombia from eastern Venezuela, began the liberation of New Granada. Four years earlier he had tried to free Venezuela, using Colombia as his base. Now he was about to succeed by reversing his direction. The great days of his military genius, his liberation, and his fame were now before him. Out of the dark thoughts of exile came one of the greatest and most difficult campaigns in all military history, a campaign which ended in the liberation of half the Latin American continent. Military success swept into Colombia from the eastern *llanos* of Venezuela. A new generation of Colombian leaders joined Bolívar and fought by his side. The greatest of patriotic intoxicants was near at hand: independence.

FOUR

A NATION AND ITS FORCES

To 1900

Francisco de Paula Santander was vice-president of Gran Colombia under Bolívar, and he became the president of a completely independent Colombia in 1832, after Bolívar died. Santander represents the first national Colombian figure of the nineteenth century. When he took office under the Angostura constitution of 1819, great changes were in the offing. One of them was the Riego liberal uprising in Spain in 1820, which cut off that nation's military power. Although the uprising in Spain did not affect the political side of South American independence, it brought about an armistice in Colombia. The Spanish revolution of 1820-23 also made possible the liberation of Antonio Nariño. (Nariño returned to Colombia in 1823 but died soon after as a result of his long imprisonment.) Santander had defeated Nariño for the vice-presidency, as the old patriot made way for the new generation.

Colombia as a Nation

Colombia's first constitution, the constitution of Cúcuta of 1812, established a new Latin American nation.[1] The new republic of Gran Colombia not only integrated the four colonies of the viceroyalty, but also continued colonial agencies. National government was as central-

[1] William M. Gibson, *The Constitutions of Colombia* (Durham, 1948).

ized as the older viceroyalty had been. Government was organized along *unitario* lines, with departments (not states) subdivided into provinces, cantons, and parishes. Even the Spanish intendancy was kept; the intendant was the head of the department, appointed by the president and ratified by the senate. Six departments were created in 1821 in the enormous territory of Gran Colombia. The Spanish colonial *cabildo* was now merged with its suburbs and called a *canton*.

Centralism was the supporting twin of nationalism, since congress was empowered over the authority of the department to regulate "their number, boundaries, and powers as well as anything else which may be conducive to their better administration." This centralized character of the first Colombian government was also evident in its power to declare war, to collect taxes, and to pass laws, as well as in the authority and leadership of President Bolívar and Vice-President Santander. The capital was fixed at Bogotá.

Colombia's early liberalism also appears in this constitution of 1821. In contrast to the 1811 constitution of the United Provinces of New Granada, which had specifically provided for the authority and establishment of the Roman Catholic Church, the 1821 constitution of Gran Colombia said nothing about the Church or any ecclesiastical authority. Perhaps it was because ten years of struggle against Spain had led to a reaction against the Church so closely identified with Spanish imperialism. On the other hand, the influence of Bolívar carried on the anticlericalism of the Venezuelan constitution of 1811, which abolished many Church privileges. The Colombian constitution of 1821 was essentially secular, especially when compared with the constitution of 1830, in which conservatives and clericals established exclusive guarantees for the Church. Liberalism and conservatism already clashed over the bitter Church-State question which was to rend Colombia for years.

The constitution also moved in the direction of civil liberties. Negro slave children were declared free at birth (as in Antioquia in 1814), but slavery was not totally abolished until 1851. Legislation abolished the Indian poll tax. Laws provided for the division of collectively owned Indian lands in order to promote ownership and use of private property. Other laws, reflecting the aspiration for wider mass education provided for elementary schools in cities and towns. The creole

program of 1821 had a distinctly liberal character akin to the liberalism in Europe, the United States, and elsewhere in Latin America at
that time. Equally important was the civilian character of the government. Also, congress had a large liberty of debate in its sessions. Bolívar only came to Cúcuta to take his oath of office, then left for the
battlefield. He rarely returned to Colombia.

A major action of Bolívar, as his armies moved southward against
the Spanish armies in Peru and Bolivia, was the annexation and in-
corporation of the Pacific port of Guayaquil (Ecuador) as a department under the central administration of Gran Colombia. Guayaquil
had valuable shipyards and maritime facilities and great commercial
importance. It was at Guayaquil that Bolívar secured the withdrawal
of the famous Argentine general, José de San Martín. Their Guayaquil Interview of 1822 is one of the most famous and mysterious con-
versations in Latin America's history. No one knows the nature of this
private talk.

Back at Bogotá, Santander confronted the struggles between departments and the federal government. An unending chain of differences, which were to last throughout history, began with a minor
clash over the choice of Bogotá instead of Caracas as the national
capital. Grievances were loudly proclaimed against the use of New
Granadan blood and money to liberate distant places like Peru and
Bolivia. Conservatives and clericals resented the new religious liberty
and the failure to make the Roman Catholic Church the official
church. The federalists demanded that the province, instead of the
centrally controlled and appointed department, become the basis for
local rights and "home rule," because the president appointed the
intendants, but the senators and deputies of congress were elected in
the provinces.

In 1826 Bolívar was in Bolivia, installing a constitution which
shocked Colombians. He had been away from Bogotá for five years.
A veteran campaigner and a military man, his military experiences
strengthened his belief in centralized government and a powerful
executive until such time as education and moral progress might jus-
tify wider suffrage and representation. The Bolivian constitution reflected his concept of a president who held office for life. It also provided a system of limited and indirect electors who were tribunes,

senators, and censors. Executives, called *censors*, were made part of the legislature; they too held office for life. As he rode northward he persuaded city after city on the way to endorse the Bolivian constitution and grant him almost dictatorial powers. His critics in Bogotá preferred to uphold their liberal constitution of 1821. A clash was imminent.[2]

More and more the two men, Bolívar and Santander, drew upon themselves the admiration or the bitter hatred of their contemporaries. In the summer of 1828, events followed one another in rapid succession, culminating in the conspiratorial outbreak against Bolívar's life in September. After the failure of the assassination attempt, Bolívar assumed an open dictatorship. Santander was accused of responsibility for the attempted crime and was tried and sentenced to death, but Bolívar accepted a council's decision to exile him to Europe.

Multinational Gran Colombia soon succumbed to civil struggles in the south and east. The Liberator's great public powers and his very considerable military prestige did not stop the swift pace of regionalism and opposition from expelling his lieutenants from Bolivia, Peru, Ecuador, and even Venezuela. He had previously promised to hold his dictatorial powers only until the meeting of another constitutional convention in 1830. But it was too late by then. Venezuela had already indicated its secession and independence; now Quito broke away. Bolívar's own wasting illness, the civil war, and the conspiracy and failure were now too much for him. In March 1830 he resigned the presidency. Then came the announcement of the secession of Colombia. A new president was chosen: Joaquín Mosquera. In June 1830, Bolívar learned that Antonio José de Sucre, his friend and aide from Venezuela through all the intense years, had been as-

[2] Nearly all Bolívar's writings are by now in several collections. There are modern biographies, one by Gerhard Masur (1948), another by Waldo Frank (1951), and that by Salvador de Madariaga (1952). Victor Andrés Belaunde studied Bolívar's political ideas in his *Bolívar and the Political Thought of the Spanish American Revolution* (Baltimore, 1958). The most useful collections of letters are in Vicente Lecuna, *Cartas del Libertador*, 10 vols. (Caracas: 1929-30); Daniel F. O'Leary, *Memorias del General O'Leary*, 32 vols. (Caracas, 1879-88); José F. Blanco and R. Azpurua, *Documentos para la Historia del Libertador de Colombia*, 14 vols. (Caracas; 1875-78); and the *Archivo Santander*, 24 vols. (Bogotá, 1913-32).

sassinated. When that year of political death closed, Bolívar died, too, in December 1830.

After Bolívar: Santander

Mosquera's presidency lasted for two years. After that, in 1832, Santander returned to Colombia from New York to become president. Colombia's history as an independent nation begins in 1833 with President Francisco de Paula Santander.[3] His government, under a centralized administration, obtained its freedom but inherited all the troubles, losses, debts, and enmities of a generation of civil and foreign wars. Santander's republic established the supremacy of the civilian over both military and ecclesiastical elements. He was a stern figure, legal-minded and inflexible. He had his own favorites; most of his enemies were Bolívar's former followers. Politically, he continued to reduce the provincial legislatures to debating societies concerned with the excessive national powers held in Bogotá. Nevertheless, although almost prostrate beneath the department and the intendant, the province continued to fulfill states' rights, needs, and local pride.

Troublesome Issues: Economic

The presiding officer of the convention of 1832 stated:

> The effort has been made in this Constitution to assure the importance of the Provinces by establishing in them a House to look after provincial interests, supervise provincial establishments, promote industry, encourage education, and participate in the selection of provincial and national officers. Henceforth centralism shall no longer be an obstacle to the felicity of the towns and the prosperity of each of them shall now be in the hands of their immediate agents.[4]

Economic issues often awakened differences of interest between the provinces and Bogotá. Clear examples of the rivalry between sectional and national influences are found in such matters as the ownership, grant, or sale of the public lands know as *baldíos*. (The *baldío* question is still very much alive in Colombia.) Local property-owners

[3] David Bushnell, *The Santander Regime in Gran Colombia* (Newark, 1954), is a dependable life-and-times biography.

[4] Gibson, *op. cit.*, pp. 117.

desired these lands when they were available in their vicinity. Very often they held them illegally, renting them out or allowing squatters to occupy them. Lawsuits and disputes were plentiful whenever the national government asserted its own claim to title, based upon national sovereignty. Bogotá issued decrees and made administrative decisions about the lands which aroused local and provincial economic interests. Many grants promised great local profits through promotion, speculation, and settlement.[5]

Another economic matter was the tariff question. The legislature's tariff laws affected and controlled the commercial, middleman role of the Caribbean cities of Cartagena and Santa Marta. Congress determined these matters according to the constitution and by statute, but the political power of Bogotá had much to do with the tariff policy. Bogotá, for example, "imported" most of her commercial needs from Cartagena. Both cities had a common interest in lowering the costs of imports and exports and in enlarging the business of merchants, brokers, river boatmen and others. They lived off trade and cared little about local manufactures or so-called infant industries. Both Bogotá and Cartagena opposed high tariffs and protectionism. High tariffs at best could offer protection to a few small factories and household industries while stimulating local smuggling and illegal trade, thus creating losses in both private and public income.

Troublesome Issues: Church and State

Economics was obscured by the Church-State controversy, army dissatisfaction, and the rise of Colombian conservatism during the next generation. The violence of the disputes between Liberals and Conservatives either simmered or boiled over into revolt from 1838 to 1878. The election of 1838 was thrown into congress to be settled. Congress chose José Ignacio de Márquez, former secretary to President Mosquera, to succeed Santander. Santander had reduced the army's influence and numbers and initiated certain reforms. He had agreed in 1834 for New Granada, Venezuela, and Ecuador, acting as separate nations, to liquidate the national debt of Gran Colombia.

[5] James J. Parsons, *Antioqueño Colonization in Western Colombia* (Berkeley, 1949), Ibero-Americana Series Number 32, Chap. 6, pp. 72-86, and Chap. 7, "Public Land Policies."

But the New Granada congress refused to agree to his assumption of 50 per cent of the obligation, based upon New Granada's larger population and wealth and her ability to pay. Congress did not ratify the agreement on the basis of population, insisting that payments be shared according to wealth. The incoming President Márquez had to settle this question.

Troublesome Issues: The Land Question

Márquez opened the era of clerical revolt by secularizing several church missions belonging to powerful religious orders. He drastically reformed the rather inactive Church policy of Santander. This explained why former followers of Bolívar gave their support to Márquez. His Church reforms were limited to dedicating mission property to educational and religious purposes. But he had the misfortune to awaken the repressed clerical and anticlerical struggle which, like liberalism and conservatism, ran deeply through the whole history of the country. In some respects, what started the struggle was his transferral of properties and control from the monasteries to the parishes, from the regular to the secular clergy. The Archbishop of Bogotá, leading generals, and ex-Presidents Mosquera and Santander supported him.

Religious tension and unrest took place in a period of economic prosperity. Cartagena recovered some of her advantages under the trade treaty with Spain in 1839. The Caribbean port could now again trade with Cuba as well as with Spain, although in rather smaller volume than her commerce of colonial days. Government revenues from customs and taxes began to increase. The internal debt was reduced. A small amount of national manufacturing had begun to develop in glassware and paper. It is worth noticing that the agreements of 1839 which permitted imports from Spain and Cuba had a retarding effect upon local industry. The New Granadan liberals as well as conservatives failed to protect infant industries. Imports and exports provided more government income than national industry could. Only a slight, unimportant difference separated liberals from conservatives over economic matters.

During the 1840's, conservative and clerical reaction had set in in many places in Latin America. This was the era of Rosas in Argentina, Santa Anna in Mexico, and Portales in Chile. It is easier to understand how Colombia echoed this wave of Metternichean reaction. The "holy alliance" between conservatives and clericals protected the Church while retaining the age-old Spanish regalist-nationalist policy of keeping the State in charge of the Church. By this time Santander had died. Pedro Herrán and Tomás de Mosquera shared the presidency up to 1850 in a decade during which "the opposition who called themselves Liberals now began to apply the name *Conservatives*." [6] The era of Herrán and Mosquera led across the sharp rocks to one of the peaks of the clerical-liberal struggle. The law of 1842, bitterly but unsuccessfully opposed, had readmitted the Jesuits.

The conservative Mariano Ospina Rodríguez, cabinet minister from 1840 to 1845, gave his country's growth a strong push. He was not a reactionary and did not blindly admire everything feudal, colonial, traditional, or Hispanic. He opposed the second generation of Colombian liberals and he certainly fought the new generation of radicals, but he also held modern views. Perhaps it was because he also administered the country when the railways and coffee were coming to influence the national economy. The country had to face the challenges of modern inventions and foreign markets. Mariano Ospina had been presiding officer of the Antioquia legislature, where he had great influence. He did a great deal to carry out those new land policies which gave Colombian public lands to private proprietors and to land companies. Ospina helped give direction to an historic frontier and settlement movement in the upper Cauca river valley, which stimulated an *antioqueño* migration to southern and southwestern Colombia. "Squatter sovereignty" struggles against the big land owners and company speculators only briefly held back this internal colonization. The chartered land companies were too strong. Conservatives in Antioquia, led by Mariano Ospina, supported this land-grant program.

The Bogotá government, before and after Ospina became president, was considerably influenced by those provincial and regional interests which were identified with the grant of private ownership to land-colonization companies. The sale or rent of these vast leagues of land

[6] Mary W. Williams, *People and Politics of Latin America*, rev. ed. (Boston, 1945), p. 527.

was authorized. Some of these *baldío* lands, as indicated, were already occupied. Often the new owners ejected the tenants or squatters. Mutual indignation among squatters and landlords was bound to spill over into political violence. The landowners were close to the conservatives in national government at Bogotá and approved the grant of Colombian national (public) lands to private, incorporated landlords.

Conservatives and Liberals: I

Conservatism, however, lost out to liberalism during the next quarter-century. Moderate liberalism at first, then more extreme liberalism, and then the victorious radicals took over the machinery of government. The prototype of moderate liberalism was Tomás de Mosquera, who was president from 1830 to 1832, from 1845 to 1849, and again before 1867. Mosquera always considered himself a moderate sort of liberal and a national rather than a partisan figure (he had fought with Bolívar), but he certainly did also represent an element of conservatism. He was the brother of the influential Archbishop of Bogotá, and came from a wealthy and aristocratic family. His liberalism probably came more from his wide travels and his sense of nineteenth century material development than from any sympathy with anticlericalism. By 1850, popular democracy, radicalism, and Utopian socialism had begun to enter Colombia, probably from the direction of France and the revolution of 1848. The liberals, as enemies of the conservatives, were now joined by the radicals. The radicals were those who upheld the concept of the natural rights of man expressed during the French Revolution. They felt that constitutional and moderate liberalism was too slow, too legal to get anywhere.

José Hilario López was the prototype of the more extreme liberal who reached over to touch radicalism. Elected in mid-century by the votes of liberals as well as those of radicals, President José López moved energetically towards greater liberty of thought, ideas, and opinions. Automatic reverence for established institutions no longer influenced the new minds. They wanted to reform education, thought, and society. Some of the radicalism was romantic, patriotic, and idealist; some of it was anticlerical; the rest pointed toward greater representation, equality, and democracy. President López did a great deal to satisfy all his supporters.

In 1851 López signed the measure which altogether abolished slavery in Colombia. He extended freedom of the press and guaranteed personal rights and privileges. He brought together the new constitutional convention of 1853, which granted male suffrage and complete religious freedom. For provincial liberals and states' righters who wanted more self-government, López signed the law of 1850, which decentralized the levying and collection of taxes. It allowed the provinces to raise funds and share a greater amount of income with the Bogotá government. López also restored or granted powers to states and towns. In 1850 another law transferred treasury contributions to the Roman Catholic Church from Bogotá by authorizing the provinces henceforth to contribute that money from their own public funds.

The tariff created another difference in the economic interests of moderate liberals and the conservatives on one hand, and the more extreme liberals and the radicals on the other. Mosquera, in order to help the merchants of Cartagena and the importers of Bogotá as well as the conservative agrarians, had taken measures after 1847 to reduce the import duties. As elsewhere in Latin America, particularly in Argentina and Mexico, this action opened the door to a flood of cheap, manufactured goods from the factories of Britain. The lowering of tariffs hit especially the household craftsmen, spinners, and weavers and the small industries of the *comunero* country at Socorro. British trade enriched importers but put small manufacturers out of business or up against the wall. López saw this situation but was not able to settle it. His attention to economic matters was drawn off by the Church-State struggles.

López, and those who followed him from 1850 to 1880, stressed the Church question, very much as did the Mexican, Benito Juarez. But the Colombian reform went even further than the Mexican reform. On May 21, 1850, the López government expelled the Jesuits, giving the same reasons as had been given in the Pragmatic Sanction of Charles III back in 1767. The next year Church tithes were abolished. Church *fueros* (privileges and exemptions), including the privilege of

separate Church courts, were made null and void. In 1853 his successor signed the law providing for the separation of Church and State
in Colombia. Civil war broke out almost instantly. It was clearly
understood at the time, moreover, that a liberal president would
never have any liberty under a conservative constitution: the next
step was a liberal constitution in 1853.

Until it was swept away by the conservative constitution of 1886,
this liberal charter of 1853 was the first step in a series of reforms of
basic constitutional practices. The liberal document of 1853 and
another liberal constitution in 1863 were intended to secure the
liberal basis of Colombian political organization. These two halves of
the constitutional whole sum up the essential aims of the liberals of
Colombia before 1920. In order to go this far, much of the localism
and states' rightism was left to the conservatives. The liberals were
the ones who now saw the need for a stronger central government.

The liberals, however, made up as they were of differing elements,
very often were weakened by their own supporters. A riotous scene
took place in 1854 when workers and their employers urged the
lower legislative house to repeal the low tariff of 1847. They brought
pressure to raise customs duties and lay a protective tariff on articles
which competed with their small industries. The moderate liberals
had clung to the principle of free trade. Industry, the radicals, and the
workers had already begun to ask for greater state intervention to
protect national interests as well as their own private ones. Street
clashes of workers added to the atmosphere of agitation and the
omen of trouble ahead. Some propaganda on behalf of the "common
man" circulated in the Bogotá garrisons. A confused revolution in
1854 gave power briefly to the soldiers, but the combined leadership
of four ex-presidents—Herrán, Márquez, López, and Mosquera—
restored civilian authority.

Modernization of the Country

When Mariano Ospina Rodríguez became president (1857-60),
Colombia was already experiencing the effects of nineteenth century
liberal ideas of progress in science, commerce, internal improvements,
and education. Liberalism had broadened in scope beyond its earlier
anticlericalism. The whole idea of progress, change, and moderniza-

tion was increasingly reflected in liberalism, while the new fact of technological growth was entering into the life of the country. Population movement and resettlement in Antioquía, for example, gave rise to new cities as well as to political shifts. The commercial city of Medellín, in the province of Antioquía, already displayed that spirit of modern profit and manufacturing zeal which made it into the so-called Manchester of South America, because of its leadership in textile weaving. Population and capital flowed into this region and further south into the upper Cauca valley.

Cali, using Buenaventura on the Pacific as its ocean port, grew from a small town into a city. At Cali the commercial classes became attached to the liberal cause to offset the clericalism and conservative aristocracy still found at Popayán. By the middle of the century, coffee planting began to move westward from Bogotá to Antioquía. Landowners and coffee growers began to call for a railway, in addition to river routes to carry out their coffee. King Coffee shared his nineteenth century throne between Bogotá and Antioquía, although it has moved again since that time. A national census was taken in 1851 and showed that the population, isolated and showing only a slight increase over 1810, was estimated at 2,040,054. (It is about fourteen million a century later.)

Other changes were the introduction of steam navigation on the Magdalena and Cauca Rivers. Steam navigation and railway transport could end the provincialism and isolation of many parts of Colombia, but geography and custom still encouraged a great deal of remoteness. Highways and railroads only slowly covered over the old pack-mule trails. Bogotá was one of the major beneficiaries of improvements in transport and communication, but Cauca and Antioquía profited as well. Steam navigation also favored Cartagena. Nevertheless, ten and more years after the mid-century, the bulk of the goods transported to the newly constructed lines still went by pack-mule or on Negro backs. Indeed, the muleteer-truckman and the Negro porter represented a vested interest which resented, opposed, and suffered economically from the coming of the railroads. These labor interests expressed themselves politically during elections and especially in their pressure upon the president and congress for protective legislation.

Conservatives and Liberals: II

The fact that a conservative was elected president in 1857 should
not be misleading; liberalism and the political effect of these economic
forces were strong: President Ospina did not serve out his term.[7]
President Ospina had taken office as an out-and-out conservative who
would not take liberals into his government and had little to do with
them. He gave no concession to the liberals, probably being convinced of conservative strength. He could not afford coalition with
liberals in view of the liberal stand on the clergy and the Church. He
outraged the liberals and even the radicals by readmitting the Jesuits
to the country. Apprehension was aroused by the dissolution of the
constitution of 1853 and the creation of a new one in 1858. The conservative-liberal clash broke out in violence again and shook the
whole country until Mosquera took Bogotá in July 1861.

One of the first acts of the liberals was to nationalize (or federalize)
the city of Bogotá, making it into a federal district (like Washington,
Mexico City, or Buenos Aires). Again the Jesuits were expelled,
religious property was secularized, and some ecclesiastical activity was
suppressed. The vehicle for liberal principles was the Rionegro constitution of 1863, which lasted almost twenty-five years (to 1885). It
was the longest period of liberal leadership in the country's history. A
curious and almost absurd provision reduced the term of the president
to two years! Fear of radicalism or democracy expressed itself in a
cautious provision that the president be elected by the states through
an electoral college, with each state possessing one vote.

This constitution of 1863 revealed some advanced political ideas. It
gave unlimited freedom of speech, guarantees of the individual, and
an unusually large grant of states' rights. The constitution also assured
freedom of worship, gave guarantees to property, and declared the
supremacy of the law. It also introduced a basis for the reform and
improvement of public education. The constitution of 1863 was one
of the most unusual expressions of liberalism to be found anywhere in
Latin America at that time.

A most important single piece of legislation was the measure of

[7] Another Mariano Ospina was the Conservative Acting President from 1948
to 1950. Bernstein, Modern and Contemporary Latin America, pp. 666-669.

1867 which created a national university with professional schools. This made possible the separation of elementary education from the university. By 1880 the liberals were able to create a minister of public education with cabinet rank.

Politics, rather than the constitution, made these reforms possible. The radicals, who are not to be considered as either social-minded or reformist in the present-day sense, were strong on anticlericalism. They also represented the shopkeepers, the workers, and the professional and business people. Those small manufacturers who looked for tariff protection also supported the radicals. A large number of left-wing liberals also worked with the radicals to get votes. On the other hand, an ever-present faction of middle-of-the-road or moderate liberals acted from time to time as independents and joined with conservatives to prevent drastic and rapid change. Liberals did not like to see central government too weak and frequently collaborated with conservatives against overdecentralization. When it came to the Church, however, the liberals almost always worked with the radicals and ignored the conservatives. For most of the time before 1886, when liberalism began to decline, Colombian politics were influenced by a coalition of doctrinaire radicals and right-wing liberals, whose leader was Dr. Rafael Núñez.

Most of the liberals' constitutional provisions and the liberal-radical congressional policies had become law before 1880. Liberal-radical republicans gave an energetic charge to Colombian life between 1863 and 1886, at which time a break occurred and the conservatives and right-wing liberals fused into a national party, forerunner of the accord of the present.

In 1880 a powerful figure, Dr. Rafael Núñez, entered the political scene, vigorously following a program of unity and order. He pushed the liberals off the stage, and they remained an obscure minority for the next fifty years. The great era of liberalism had come and gone between 1853 and 1888, not to come back again until after the depression of 1929 and the liberals' return to power in 1936. Núñez himself only held power to 1894, when he died, but the conservatives never relinquished their leadership after that. Colombia closed the nineteenth century and opened the twentieth on the note of conservatism.

Rafael Núñez was a journalist and politician. He had been a socialist-radical who had changed his opinions. Born in Cartagena in 1825, he was intellectual, widely traveled, and a good writer. After his radical years he had become an independent, then a moderate right-wing liberal who distrusted and opposed the radicals. In 1876, the radicals repaid him by using their votes in congress to defeat his bid for the presidency. That political fact was hidden in the bloodshed of the conservative rebellion of that year. The radicals would have nothing to do with him and it was with conservative support that he finally became president in 1880.

During this first term of office Núñez read, wrote, and spoke on the virtues of national unity, religious toleration, internal peace, and the high patriotism of his conservative and right-wing liberal supporters. Núñez reconciled moderate liberalism and conservatism. He brought together the leading elements of politics and society in a coalition similar to that which exists today. His new nationalism was called *Regeneración*. His own liberals and the conservatives put down their opponents, allied themselves in the National Party, and ushered in the new and long era of conservatism.

The Núñez constitution of 1886 remained in effect until 1936 and sent liberalism into eclipse. It increased the president's term from two years to six. Núñez' Regeneración dominated legislative practices. No liberal uprising or civil opposition was able to shake off conservative rule after Núñez had laid its new base. Not only liberalism, but even the nineteenth century issues of federalism and states' rights receded from view during the next half-century.

States were again reduced to departments, subordinate to what the constitution called a "unitary republic." The states were even ignored in the ratification of the constitution: it was passed on the votes of city councils. The constitution, which came into effect during Núñez' second presidential term, recognized the national government at Bogotá as the source of all the public powers.

Núñez, the former radical, provided conservatism and clericalism in Colombia with one of its most adroit and accomplished leaders. He may not have had the attractive civil and aristocratic mind of Mariano Ospina, but his appeal to popular opinion and his knowledge of practical politics, were undoubtedly greater. Like Santa Anna of

Mexico, Rafael Núñez, under the excuse of illness, spent a great deal of his time at his home in Cartagena. He, too, allowed his vice-president to prepare and sign legislation. It is ironic that Cartagena, the home of much Colombian regionalism and the capital of strong international commercial interest, should have given Colombia one of her most conservative and centralizing presidents.

The Regeneration and the Return of the Church

Rafael Núñez restored to the Church practically all her former influence and power. The Church was again brought back into the State and made the official religion. Yet there was some desire not to provoke the anticlericalism always latent in Colombia. The Roman Catholic Church was the religion of the nation, but the constitution added that the Church "is not and shall not be an established Church and it shall preserve its independence." This arrangement greatly resembled that made in Italy. The Church was given control over public education. Some gain was made in religious toleration by providing for the activity of small sects, chiefly Protestant. The constitution allowed "the practice of all cults not contrary to Christian morals or law." This provision came to be interpreted as "subversive of the public order," and is still considered to embody a clear and present danger to society and morals.

The acts of the Núñez era were much more important than the general language of the constitution. Once again the Jesuits were brought back; they are still there and have built up considerable influence. Many other religious orders were reinstated and some new ones were introduced. Núñez' most important religious action was the concordat with the Vatican, ratified in February 1888. This treaty was basic to the effectiveness of all other measures taken on behalf of Church aims. The concordat of 1888 provided in part for the Colombian government to make financial contributions to the Church, to pay for previously confiscated Church property, and to recognize the religious orders. The concordat of 1888 was supplemented by another in 1948, which carried on the patterns of Church and State interests.

The concordat and the Núñez Regeneración conferred great powers upon the Catholic Church in matters of education. Religious—i.e.,

Catholic—teaching was made compulsory in schools, colleges, and university. Education was to be carried on in accordance with the dogmas and morals of the Church. The *imprimatur* of the Archbishop of Bogotá was required for all school texts having to do with morals and ethics. Since morals, as a field, included education, family, welfare, and children as well as behavior, it is clear that the concordat gave the Church an extremely wide area of control over ideas. Colombian liberals objected to the concordat, but the combination of conservatives and nationalists was too strong. Colombia returned to almost full colonial orthodoxy. Núñez led Colombia as close as he could to the open theocracy and Church control which had dominated neighboring Ecuador.

Núñez' skill in balancing local federalism with feudalism guaranteed the longest period of Conservative rule. He also forced a national and central government upon Colombia. He was re-elected to a third term in 1892, but his death in 1894 interrupted anything further he might have done. There were more Liberal tests and even uprisings, the worst of them lasting from 1899 to 1903. But Núñez had fixed conservative principles so firmly that not even the science-minded doctrine of Positivism made the mark on Colombia that it did on Mexico, Brazil, Chile, and Argentina. Only the new liberalism and, after 1930, social-minded radicalism could replace his legacy.

Panama

With the turn of the twentieth century, it appeared that conservatives' values of order, tradition, Hispanic culture, Catholicism, and strong government would keep their control. But a new force for dissent and disunity emerged from another direction: an independent Panama and the Canal route. The historic Colombian division over sectionalism had resulted some concessions in the constitution of 1886, intended to mollify local and Liberal demands. It did not take long for regionalism to awaken dormant secessionist and patriotic sentiments in Panama. President Núñez, during his second term of office, had resided almost continuously in his home town of Cartagena, an old commercial rival of Panama. Through his influence, Cartagena increased her domination over that whole stretch of coastal area to Panama. The fateful secession of Panama was the first major loss of

Colombian national territory since the disintegration of Gran Colombia in 1830. It resulted as much from internal rivalries and the political civil wars as it did from Panamanian patriotism or the aggressive actions of President Theodore Roosevelt of the United States.

FIVE

EARLY TWENTIETH-CENTURY HISTORY

Panama was lost just at the end of another disastrous civil war in 1903 between liberals and conservatives. President Rafael Reyes, a strong man, preserved national unity during his term of office (1904-10). His centralist rule brought considerable material change and improvement. As nineteenth-century questions of sectionalism and ecclesiasticism were settled, economic and social matters moved onto the foreground.

Banking, paper money, tariffs, the slowly growing textile industry, coffee exports, public works, railways, and even the beginning labor question demanded attention. In the opening years of the twentieth century, the Colombian government began to find the time and money to challenge problems of the environment—the high mountain ranges and the natural isolation of many parts of the country. Bogotá, although the political capital, was still distant from and even inaccessible to many parts of the country.

Coffee, Oil, and Other Products

The isolation of the highland region in which Bogotá was located was slowly overcome by modern facilities. The conservative administrations which followed the Reyes presidency understood the need to promote economic advance in different areas. Political and economic forces were both stimulated. In southern Colombia, for example, the traditional sway of aristocratic, Catholic, and conservative Popayán now increasingly encountered the challenge of commercial, middle-class, and Liberal Cali. By 1914, the road which connected Cali to the Pacific port city of Buenaventura was opened to traffic; that same year, the new Panama Canal was opened too. Cali grew continuously and became one of Colombia's major cities.

Cali was then the chief outlet for the coffee of Antioquia and Caldas, and the point of entrance for other wealth in the southern regions. With the rise of importance of coffee and Medellín textiles, Cali overtook Cartagena. Moreover, the discovery of oil at different points along the Caribbean spurred the city of Barranquilla to a new commercial importance. Cartagena, the home of Núñez and the once-famed "Gibraltar of the Indies," entered into a serious decline from which it has never really recovered.

The emergence of coffee as the economic basis of agriculture and landowning best explains the reason for economic progress during the long Conservative epoch of the present century. The coffee plant took admirably to the slopes and plateaus of the very same Andean ranges which were barriers to transportation and communication. Coffee zones arose and flourished best on the Cundinamarca plateau at Bogotá or north of it at Norte de Santander (near the famous battleground at Cúcuta). Before 1914, the eastern Andean slopes or plateau districts produced most of the coffee crop. Since then coffee has moved west and southwest to Caldas, Antioquia, and nearby zones.

When coffee production was chiefly located in eastern-central Colombia, the political influence of the Conservative planter was strongly felt in Bogotá. Colombian railway and communication lines obeyed the rules of political centralism as well as those of geography and profits: most of the railways were merely spurs and branch lines intended to reach the Magdalena River where the coffee bags were floated downriver. This was far cheaper than the involved and costly engineering necessary to construct railways direct to the Caribbean. Puerto Berrío on the Magdalena was the main river port for the western-central city of Medellín. The coffee routes coincided with the main political artery of the country, although small, short-haul lines often ran out to plantations from Cúcuta, Barranquilla, and other distant growing centers. Coffee paid the freight rates and revenues of these lines.

During the Reyes era, most of the railway lines were franchised to the Magdalena River. After 1914, both coffee and railway transport migrated west to Manizales and Cali, in the upper Cauca valley. After 1941, more than 60 per cent of coffee exports left Colombia by the southwestern Cali-Buenaventura route, rather than by the river.

It must be made clear that these *antioqueño* planters remained conservative in their politics even though they urged, and paid for, technological and material progress. Although most advocates of such scientific change in Latin America embraced the "sociology" of Positivism, the Colombians did not. However, in spite of their clericalism and conservatism, the creoles of Antioquía made good use of their political party to push for public works, internal improvements, and other types of national government assistance. Their sectional pride was not hurt. The *antioqueños* had a sure hand for the practical and economic side of things, whether they were wealthy planters or businessmen and capitalists.

Conservatives and Liberals: III

During the years from 1900 to 1929, neither liberals nor conservatives gave much thought to contemporary social problems of labor, socialism, agrarianism, or Indianism. Colombia had, seemingly, worn itself out over clericalism and federalism. It had no energy or interest in twentieth century issues of labor, reform, and revolution. Fortunately for the leading parties and the country, there was little need for any up-to-date social philosophy: the labor movement was trifling in size and strikes were rare.

No Marxist socialism or anarchist syndicalism was evident. The Indian question in Colombia was unaffected by the Mexican Revolution of 1917 or the Andean APRA movement arising in Peru about that same time. Labor, Indian, radical, or socialist ideas had hardly any form or expression in Colombia before 1920. Manufacturing, capitalism, and the production of coffee, oil, and bananas nurtured labor's rise only after 1920, and even then very slowly. For most of the period from 1900 to 1920, coffee formed the basis for a patriarchal feudalism. Then, between 1920 and 1930, oil and textiles brought a Colombian working class into existence.

Conservative political "coalition" with liberalism went hand in hand with this era of industrial peace and progress. It must be remembered that such political and civic unity was imposed by force of arms. The need for internal security and for the defense of a Conservative society cost as much or perhaps more than railway construction or public improvements. The costs of Colombian government grew as both the size of the regular army and the amount of public construction expanded. President Reyes was careful not to practice false economy by discharging any army officers or reducing their salaries. The Colombian army began to occupy a more and more important place in national affairs. The supremacy of Conservatives, clericals, and the military cost the Colombian nation vast sums. The resulting effect was a prolonged inflation in which the high expenses were met by paper money emissions and further foreign loans. Fortunately, the country's credit abroad was good before 1922 because defaults on the foreign debt were too risky to attempt.

The great paper money emissions of 1899 and 1909 coincided with large expenditures upon public works and internal improvements. They show the large and directing role of the Colombian government over national economic development. Inflation also had considerable effect upon internal and foreign trade, banking policy, and the declining ratio of paper money values to gold. Colombia's gold production, one of the world's largest during three previous centuries, had fallen off greatly by the end of the Reyes era and the eve of World War I. The paradox was that foreign credit, coffee prices, and government banking credit needs kept Colombia on the gold standard even when her own gold production could not.

The Banco Nacional, authorized in the constitution of 1886, was later given vast powers to issue paper money under presidential responsibility and control. In 1905, President Reyes, seeking tighter executive authority over financial policy, merged the ministries of finance and treasury into one office. The shaky fiscal position of Colombia after the depression of 1907 compelled congress in 1909 to redeem these issues of paper money. Laws provided for the conversion of paper money to gold at a suitable ratio at which payments and redemption could be made. For the interest alone on the foreign debt, President Reyes agreed to deduct 15 per cent of the customs income and set it aside.

Reyes, who learned something from his contemporary Porfirio Diaz in Mexico, was clearly a dictator. He seemed to hold back the pull of Positivism in Colombia, while accelerating the material progress which he desired. He was a shrewd dictator—not as intellectual as Rafael Núñez, but just as astute. Reyes had little interest in or regard for constitutional government, elections, or the representative system. The Conservative oligarchy exercised its own power through its control of congress. Reyes did not succeed, as Núñez had, in forging a "National Union." Congress began to differ with him. Popular opposition also broke out, and there were several attempts upon Reyes' life. In 1909 the Colombian congress, backed by student and nationalist demonstrations, rejected the treaties which Reyes had signed with the United States and Panama. Reyes had agreed to recognize the independence of Panama and to accept $25,000,000 from the United States for "damages."

Reyes was forced to resign and to leave Colombia. A new alignment of Liberals and Conservatives appeared. It was called the Republican Union or Republican Party, to avoid the unpleasant memory of the Núñez Regeneración. The leaders then set up their coalition, and set out to govern Colombia through weak executives (the president's term was reduced to four years) and strong congresses. Liberalism was a silent partner in this successful Conservative era which lasted down to 1930.

Although domestic politics were under new control, economic and social forces were beginning to stir. World War I gave a forward push to economic progress, even though Colombia remained neutral and her foreign trade fell off. Oil and textiles emerged as leading industrial products. The textile industry, already important before the war, made great strides during the next two decades. Medellín was the center of this industry, creating a new capitalism in Antioquía, where agriculture was once so strong. Not all the rich businessmen were Liberals. Pedro Nel Ospina, a wealthy textile capitalist, became leader of the Conservatives and president of Colombia from 1922 to 1926.

After World War I

During the last years of World War I and the first postwar years, a wave of paper money issues again marked national treasury policy. Paper currency covered government expenses and helped ease the loss

of government revenues caused by a decline in imports (and, there-
fore, in taxes). In addition, subsidies to the Church and Society of
Jesus and the annual payments to the Vatican stipulated in the
Concordat also drained the government budget.

From 1920 to 1940, new social and economic changes in labor,
industry, and intellectual doctrines challenged this entrenched Con-
servative-Church leadership. A resurgent and new Liberalism, an
emerging trade unionism, and a Socialist Party (soon to divide into a
Communist faction) brought Colombia face to face with the issues
of the twentieth century. A new and dynamic capitalism, bent upon
the industrialization of Colombia, also tested the relations between
capital, labor, and government.

At the end of the war Colombia experienced the usual wave of
strikes against low wages, inflated prices and rents, and shortages of
food and goods. The Conservatives and the Republican Union
Liberals passed legislation in 1918 which allowed the national government to intervene in capital-labor disputes to promote and protect
public health, morals, and safety. But the Conservative administration
refused to raise wages or lower prices since such an action would have
interfered with the liberty of industry and freedom of enterprise.
Nevertheless, that mild legislation of 1918 was the earliest Colombian
precedent for expression of government concern for the workers' welfare.

The strikes of 1917 and 1918, with the examples of the Mexican
and Russian Revolutions before them, induced the Conservatives to
accept these unwelcome measures. The laws regulated only the dangers to health and safety, saying nothing about the basic issues of
wages, employment, trade union recognition, or collective bargain-
ing. In some respects, Colombian Conservatism took to heart and followed the new Catholic expressions of social justice as already proclaimed by the Pope. Another Conservative measure which this time
struck fire from the business and manufacturing classes was the levying of an income tax, even though it was low, limited in coverage,
and with large areas for exemptions. A start was also made in the
direction of slum clearance and the construction of workers' houses.

The postwar administration of Pedro Nel Ospina (1922-26) inherited the problems of unemployment, suspension of public works,
and other symptoms of a depressed economy. This wealthy Conserva-

tive industrialist took up the stabilization of finances and credit reforms "from the top down," instead of initiating social improvements "from the bottom up." The United States banking mission, headed by Princeton Professor E. W. Kemmerer, made recommendations which were strongly denounced by critics. One change provided for a more centralized banking system and the creation of the national Banco de la Republica. The Banco was authorized to introduce and control branch banking in the several departments. Forty years later, in November 1963, the government instituted a Monetary Board, with powers similar to those of the United States Federal Reserve Board. The Monetary Board is empowered to deter inflation and regulate the supply of money by raising rediscount rates controlling local bank loans and credits.

Colombian issues of paper money were again condemned. The Kemmerer mission recommended adherence to the gold standard. Steps were taken to assure not only the publication of the national budget, but of a balanced one. (Just before the arrival of the Kemmerer mission, the Ospina administration had ratified the Thompson-Urrutia Treaty, which revoked the Bidlack Treaty of 1846. Colombia thereby acknowledged the independence of Panama and accepted a twenty-five million dollar indemnity from the United States. The first installment reached Colombia in late 1922, just in time to help the incoming Ospina administration.)

The Kemmerer mission made many enemies because of its recommendations and its influence upon the Ospina government. It was bitterly criticized for recommending that the government retrench and for insisting on a balanced budget. Such recommendations meant the dismissal of many government workers and bureaucratic politicians, and the reduction of the wages and salaries of those who remained. The use of funds for social benefits, schools, hospitals, and other nonrevenue-producing services was postponed indefinitely.

The Ospina administration, however, did a good deal to assist the further prosperity of the coffee planters. Ospina established the credit facility of a National Mortgage Bank under government auspices. The organized influence of the coffee interests went still further in 1927 (after Ospina's term), when the large producers established the still-powerful Federación Cafetera, a sort of lobby of the chief coffee planters of the country. Ospina also encouraged the establishment and growth of the first airline in South America, authorized in 1920. This was the German-dominated SCADTA Line (Sociedad Colombo Alemanade Transportes Aéreos). It was much enlarged after nationalization and was renamed AVIANCA. The airline brought many regions of Colombia in touch with each other and profited from international and domestic passenger traffic as well as from small bulk freight.

Between 1920 and 1930, Colombian oil enriched foreign trade, Caribbean development, and government revenues. In 1927 and 1928 Colombia adopted a policy of national control (but not ownership) of the oil industry. Foreign concessions and alien ownership played a large role during the Ospina administration and afterward. Colombia's oil economics had both geographic and political effects. The rapid growth of the Caribbean city of Barranquilla was one result. The declining influence of old Santa Marta and Cartagena now made way for dynamic Barranquilla. The port also controlled the river trade from the inland Magdalena valley.[1]

The Rise of the Left

As capital and government moved along these lines, labor and newly-born socialism revealed their own restlessness. Labor entered into trade unions and mutual benefit societies. Some trade unionists already demanded a separate political party for labor. Labor and socialist groups, very small, were both influenced by intellectuals who favored a working-class political philosophy. The small Socialist Party arose during the 1920's. Under its few intellectual leaders, it presented a program of mild, evolutionary Socialism, with special stress upon electoral changes and social improvements in land and labor. A more practical objective of workers was a program of social security. This was provided by the loose federation of groups known as the Directorio Nacional Socialista y Obrera, whose aims were chiefly welfare and benefit.

Colombian labor syndicalism, the militant counterpart of the anarchosyndicalism active elsewhere on the continent, fought this social-

[1] Harry Bernstein, *Modern and Contemporary Latin America* (Chicago, 1952), pp. 628-72. See also Arthur P. Whitaker, *The United States and South America: The Northern Republics.* American Foreign Policy Library (Cambridge, Mass., 1948), p. 55.

ist activity on one hand while launching anticapitalistic strikes on the other. Not until the later 1920's did Colombian Communist propaganda among intellectuals and workers become worth noticing. Communists, under their Social Revolutionary Party, first tried to get into the labor unions and to organize a separate Labor slate in elections. Generally speaking, the Social Revolutionary Party was an early front for the Communist International. Not until 1930 was a Colombian Communist Party formed. Between the end of World War I and the depression decade which began in 1930, Colombia slowly moved closer to the issues of working-class politics, radical activities, Communism, and the other Marxist movements of the left.

The Liberal Party also reflected the forces of the day. From about 1926 on, liberalism began to take on the colors of all the contemporary classes and movements. Some working-class groups tried to get the Liberals to incorporate planks for social security and other labor legislation. The older liberalism, still largely interested in anticlericalism, the constitution, and political questions, was called upon more and more to take the lead on behalf of the laboring classes.

Class-struggle concepts in Colombia were so dulled that employers enjoyed their workers' support at the polls. Pressure now arose to induce the Liberals to take up social and economic needs. In part this was to prevent any break between employers and workers which might lead to separate political action by labor.

The Liberals boycotted the election of 1926, which brought into office a traditionalist Conservative. The Liberal boycott made it easy for the Conservative candidate to win. The boycott indicated that Liberals continued to think more of basically political matters, leaving social and economic questions to others. The Liberal boycott extended further: the party also held out against accepting any office in the cabinet. The days of Liberal participation in the National Union of the later nineteenth century or the Republican Union of the World War I decade were gone, at least for the next generation. This time the Liberals had guessed right: they escaped all the criticism leveled the Conservatives after 1928 and during the depression years of 1929-30.

In 1930 the Socialist Party, the Liberals, and an "insurgent" wing of the Conservatives were ready to run their three separate candidates against the "regular" Conservative candidate. The prolonged Liberal boycott of presidential elections freed them from the stigma of government corruption. Any one of the three parties was likely to do something for businessmen, small towns, artisans, and workers. Each of them could reduce taxes and the cost of government and promised a badly needed design for economic recovery.

The Socialists had already begun to make progress at the polls. The year before, in 1929, they had run up an impressive vote in the Bogotá city election. A bad strike in 1928, on banana plantations owned by the North American United Fruit Company, had been forcefully suppressed by the Conservative government. Labor unions were restive and angry. New leaders, slogans, and agitation were appearing. The government reduced employment and contracts in public works, roadbuilding, and other hiring measures. Taxes remained proportionately and unduly high. The price of coffee fell dangerously low. But there was no revolutionary situation. In fact, instead of taking military action, the government permitted the presidential election to take place. But this time the Liberals decided the time was ripe to abandon their boycott. Public interest was high enough for them to enter the elections and name their own candidate. They chose a figure whose views were moderate.

Return of the Liberals

Enrique Olaya Herrera, who had been serving the Conservative president as the minister to the United States, became the victorious Liberal candidate in 1930. The Conservatives, however, retained a majority in congress. Nevertheless, this was the first presidential election the Liberals had won since 1886. Their victory was tempered by the check which Conservatives imposed upon legislation and the continued slowness with which liberalism faced the new forces of social and economic change.

Olaya Herrera had made a campaign of sorts on women's suffrage (always a true Liberal advance in Catholic countries like Colombia) and an appeal for continued investment of capital in his country and for mild economic controls. None of these remedies could cope with the mounting unemployment, the sharper demands for social legislation and security, and the increasing number of strikes. But the government moved slowly and temperately. Avoiding the specific pressure of the Colombian Socialists for the expropriation of the oil companies, both the Liberal Olaya Herrera and the Conservative Congress agreed only to declare the oil industry a public utility and to regulate it in the national interest.

Another government measure, one which indicated the importance of the Federación Cafetera, authorized the grant of loans and credits from the national treasury to the coffee planters. In the five years since its establishment in 1927 the Federación had been permitted by the government to collect a tax on each exported sack of coffee. The revenue was used to improve coffee credits, repay loans, promote sales, set up centers for agricultural research, and improve marketing arrangements.

From 1930 to 1946, the Liberals guided Colombia through economic recovery, reorganization of national education, a border war with Peru, a new settlement with the Church, reorganization of the constitution, World War II, and increased economic nationalization and industrialization. Conservative resistance always was vocal, but as a leftward tendency emerged among the Liberals, the moderate and right-wing Liberal opposition went to the other side. A new *regeneración* of National Union was repeatedly favored.[2]

Between the presidencies of Olaya Herrera (1930-34) and Alfonso López (1942-46), for example, a slowly perceptible split began to separate the traditional, political-minded Liberals from the contemporary, more social-minded Liberals. The newer Liberals began to envision a "new deal" for Colombia—the extension of national control over the economy, social security, labor, and the development of private and public capital. The depression years also brought Colombia into an age when the Socialists, Communists, Radicals and "popular fronts" all operated actively. Agitation on behalf of conservation of human and national resources rather than the conservation of private property and private religious belief was another way of putting the chief issue of the 1930's.

The press and the general public also took part in the controversy. There were three leading newspapers in Bogotá. Each had a national circulation and influence and an affirmed political position, whether Liberal or Conservative. Each was owned by a politician-publisher who eventually became president. Eduardo Santos, president from

[2] John D. Martz, *Colombia: A Contemporary Political Survey* (Chapel Hill, 1962), pp. 13-15.

1938 to 1942, was owner and publisher of the moderate *El Liberal*. Alfonso López, president from 1934 to 1938 and from 1942 to 1945, published *El Tiempo*, one of the best known Liberal journals in South America. Laureano Gómez, president from 1950 to 1953, was the publisher of the ultra-Conservative, strongly proclerical and almost fascist, *El Siglo*.

The Communist Party had been reorganized in 1930. Before Olaya Herrera could even finish out his term, a new language of left-wing politics interrupted. Socialists, labor, unions, and leftist Liberals spoke of the "revolution on the march," of Soviet Russia, Communism, and the peoples' fronts. Communists directed their agitation toward the Indians as well as toward the workers. They demanded the division of the big estates. But the Communist line and Party unity did not last long. Perennial and chronic splits again weakened Communist strength. The Colombian Federation of Labor also took a new lease on life at this time, urging trade union rights, minimum wages, and many labor reforms.

Still another kind of nationalism and political excitement aroused emotions. In 1932 the Leticia dispute between Peru and Colombia moved perilously close to war, stirring up national feelings of the more patriotic sort—and also helping to extend the power of the central government. The Salamón-Lozano Treaty, signed by Peru and Colombia in 1922 over the protest of Brazil, had given Colombia title to the upper Amazon system. Colombia received a wide stretch of land south of the Putumayo River. For exactly ten years, from 1922 to 1932, the disputed territory remained as it had always been: unpopulated, unprofitable, and unimportant.

In 1932 the little village of Leticia, in the Putumayo corridor, was invaded by an armed Peruvian band. Colombians resisted and a small-scale, "trial" war broke out. Brazil, whose interest in the Amazon Valley was considerable, had already arranged satisfactory boundary agreement with President Ospina in 1925. Peru seemed to be isolated. Under the guidance of the League of Nations commission in 1934, the disputing parties went all the way to Rio de Janeiro to negotiate. The treaty brought great credit upon the Liberals for settling an international crisis without war and for keeping Leticia as Colombian territory.

New elections took place in 1934. Olaya Herrera had managed to finish his term, holding extremists in line and getting a fair amount of middle-of-the-road unity from the Conservatives, moderate Liberals, and progressive Liberals. Even some of the Communists supported the "patriotic" war over Leticia. Olaya attempted chiefly to hold on to the national unity he had achieved, and the moderate, restrained aims of his so-called Medellín Program of 1930. All depended upon holding together the Conservatives and moderate Liberals, for he had no majority of his own. In spite of the economic questions of the day, he was zealous on behalf of old-fashioned Liberalism. His campaign platform, the Medellín Program, was a clear example of moderation in government and economics, avoiding the "new dealism" others were advocating. He spoke and wrote chiefly of efficient government and effective financial and public works policies.

But economic conditions became worse. The recovery was slow and the short struggle with Peru saddled the nation with military costs. Pressures mounted within Liberal ranks for a platform which recognized social and economic questions. In 1934 the "social question" definitely entered the Colombian scene. The Liberals won the presidential election with Alfonso López as their candidate. They were faced with two campaign commitments: continuation of traditional Liberalism in public education and regulation of the Church. They had also offered the worker, the peasant, and the left-wing intellectual agrarian reform, social security, and radical principles. To gain these objectives, in a political atmosphere charged with the social struggles of fascism, Communism, and peoples' fronts, Alfonso López and the "new Liberals" now proposed that the 1886 constitution be revised and brought up to date.[3]

[3] Vernon Fluharty, *Dance of the Millions: Military Rule and Social Revolution in Colombia*, 1930-56 (Pittsburgh, 1957), p. 212.

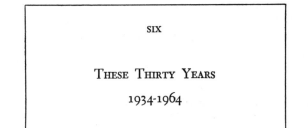

SIX

THESE THIRTY YEARS

1934-1964

The reforms of the López administration were the Colombian equivalent of the contemporary Cárdenas era in Mexico and
the Radical-Popular Front in Chile. Dr. López had dramatically transformed political aims from the past into the present. He stood
squarely for a new deal. As his term of office went on, an unofficial
"popular front" climate gave a unique character to the legislation.
Laws favored trade unionism. The Colombian Federation of Labor,
Confederación Nacional Sindical, grew stronger. A purged Communist Party, whose leader was—and is—Gilberto Vieira commended
López with reservations, first opposing then supporting him. Nearly
all his program was formulated in 1936 as a result of the amendments
of that year to the Constitution of 1886.

The Colombian López Era

López' new nationalism and liberalism was favored by the socially
minded population, but opposed by big landowners, high churchmen,
leading Conservatives and those who held office in venerable institutions such as the supreme court. The supreme court declared unconstitutional his efforts to finance his reforms by means of income tax
and capital tax. López then asked congress in 1935 to pass his program as legislated amendments to the constitution of 1886. The
Conservatives had not nominated anyone to oppose López in 1934

and now deeply regretted that boycott, using fair as well as unfair means of showing their position. López thus codified his Liberal reforms to the Constitution of 1886 without having to overthrow that Conservative charter. The codification is sometimes called the "Constitution of 1936." Not in fact a constitution, the code of laws nonetheless contains all the elements of modernization, nationalism, socialization, industrialization and agrarianism which fulfilled creole, labor, and Liberal aims.

It was not altogether extreme. Article 28 of the 1936 codification gave power to the State to intervene in the "exploitation of public and private business and industries for the purpose of ratonalizing production, distribution, and the consumption of goods, or to give labor the just protection to which it has a right." Article 40 promised labor the "special protection of the State." The code reiterated a provision for control of national expenditures by a national budget. Article 26 specifically guaranteed the right of private property, except in cases involving public utility or social interest. López did not want nationalization or socialization of property, nor did he seek to establish national ownership of national subsoil resources.

There was division among Liberals over the socioeconomic innovations. López satisfied many but aroused others with the anticlerical measures. The government acquired power to inspect public and private (i.e., parochial) schools. Once again Catholic priests were denied the privilege of running for political office. The new laws guaranteed freedom of conscience and worship. Generous legal protection of the copyright on books also won intellectual Liberals over to the new laws.

López was as national as he was liberal. He challenged the historic position of his party's liberalism on two other matters. He became a strong proponent of central government, and was cool towards any connection between states' rights and Liberalism. The codification of 1936 also ended the autonomy of the Colombian states. They were again reduced to departments, each headed by a governor appointed by the national government. The law also created *intendencias* and *comisarías*; considered to be territories, they were held under control of Congress. The first Article of the Code stated that "the Colombian nation is reconstituted a unitary republic."

The supreme court decision declaring the income tax and other tax laws unconstitutional gave a firm push to the efforts of Conservatives and moderate Liberals to combine, inside and outside of congress, against López and his reforms. Moderate and right-wing Liberals determined to wrest control of the Liberals away from López and his supporters. In 1937 the moderate Liberals increased their influence in congress and made their presence felt. The moderates intended to recall Olaya Herrera and run him as their presidential candidate in 1938, but he died. The candidate finally selected was Eduardo Santos, owner and publisher of the famous newspaper *El Liberal.* He won, and held office from 1938 to 1942. His policies were more moderate and retrenching than those of the publisher of *El Tiempo* had been. Santos and López spoke for the two wings of Liberalism.

The Santos Years

Santos curbed the Liberal-sponsored pace which seemed rushing towards radicalism. He tried to steer his Liberals back towards a more limited ambition, renewing progress in political reform and civilian liberties but playing down social and economic reforms. He did not repeal or otherwise disturb the constitutional amendments of 1936, he simply stopped introduction of any further socioeconomic legislation.

Santos established new cabinet ministries for labor, hygiene and health, social welfare, and the national economy, but his major efforts were toward business growth. He turned instead to the development of business and national economic resources under a Colombian form of "National Liberalism," convinced that aiding the growth and prosperity of business would assure labor of employment and wages. The pressure from textile interests for continued tariff protection, the need for subsidization of mining production, and the slump in the oil industry called attention to the importance of middle-class capitalism and industrialism in Colombia.

One of the ever-present cries of the middle class and of nationalistic Liberalism in the Santos era was for the creation of a Colombian iron and steel industry. Economists, business interests, journalists, and congressman all fixed upon the modern technological goal of a national steel mill. As a result of the economic planning already begun by López, President Santos signed a law passed in 1938 enabling construction of a steel mill at Medellín. The Santos government went into the steel business with some private businessmen, and the small-scale operations of the Medellín plant grew during Santos' terms of office. The Paz del Rio plant took its place in the Latin American Industrial Revolution alongside the Huachipato mill in Chile, the Chimbote in Peru, the San Nicolás in Argentina, and the Volta Redonda in Brazil.

The relative importance of manufacturing and industrialization compared to coffee and other agriculture during the business-oriented era of Santos was made public in the Censo Industrial, the Industrial Survey, of 1940. This survey showed that Colombia's largest industry in terms of investment was still textile manufacturing, largest also in point of the number of workers employed. Other national industry was engaged in food processing, drugs, brewing, sugar refining (under almost 100 per cent tariff protection), cigar and cigarette production, and an expanding shoe industry (also well protected by government high tariff). Oil, coal, and hydroelectric power supplied energy to many of these local industries.

New industries of recent years, such as chemicals, have sprung up virtually beside the handicraft shops operated by artisan owners or employing at most a handful of workers. Nevertheless, there were still more than four times as many workers on the ranches and farms as worked in the factories. An Instituto de Fomento Industrial (Industrial Development Institute) was sponsored by the Santos government, much as the coffee planters had sponsored the Federación Cafetera back in 1927. The government capitalized this Industrial Development Institute at three million dollars and received loans and economic aid from United States agencies.

The López-inspired "honeymoon" between capital and industry on the one hand and labor on the other, with the government in between, came to an end when Santos assumed office. Communism reached its peak in 1936:

> In 1936 the May First parade was a joint demonstration of organized labor, various Socialist and Communist groups, together with members of the ruling Liberals. The celebration was concluded by addresses delivered from the balcony of the presidential palace and by Gilberto Vieira, leader of the Communist Party, who stood next to the head of state and came out in support of the reformist and democratic policies of President López.[1]

[1] Stephen Naft, "Fascism and Communism in South America," *Foreign Policy Association Reports* (December 15, 1937), p. 233.

This influence waned under Santos; Communist labor had never had the power and position attributed to it in any event. In 1936, there were on the Central Committee of the Colombian Labor Federation eight moderates, four Socialists, four Communists, and one anarcho-syndicalist. When Santos finished his term in 1942, the moderation of his brand of liberalism and the wartime state of mind and economic opportunity had reduced the dangers from Labor, from the social progressivism of the liberal "left-of-center," and from the Communists.

In his politics, Santos welcomed Conservative aid to offset Liberalism's previous enthusiastic coalition with labor. Liberals, it is clear, had lost much of their effective unity because of their internal tug-of-war over the common man and the elite. Santos did uphold the civilian and congressional traditions against militarism, but he would not follow labor and left-wing Liberalism as readily as they would have had him. He sought closer ties with the United States, and general bettering of inter-American relations. He returned Colombia to the Vatican with the Concordat of 1942. He hoped that this would settle the historic religious problem and please both Liberal wings, but it satisfied them less than it did his Conservative associates.

The Vatican Pact of 1942 was signed on the eve of a new presidential campaign and amidst strong wartime tensions. The successes of the Church with Mussolini in Italy and with Franco in Spain had raised fears of fascism. Critical and secular Liberals, together with Democrats and Marxists, attacked Catholicism all the more because of the influence of the Spanish *Falange* and the propaganda of *Hispanidad* within Colombia. Although the Papacy had gone along with one aspect of Colombian nationalism—agreeing that members of the hierarchy should be, or should become, citizens of Colombia —the Pact of 1942 reawakened all the historic apprehensions and sharpened internal divisions.[2]

Alfonso López followed Santos into the presidency, his second term, and took to himself the leadership of the Liberal opposition. But the Liberals were split more deeply than ever. López never finished his second term—he dramatically resigned the presidency in 1945, a year before his term was to end.

[2] Harry Bernstein, *Modern and Contemporary Latin America* (Chicago, 1952), p. 659. This old view of Stephen Duggan is no longer held.

The New Conservativism

Two important figures emerged at this time. One was a Conservative of the deepest dye, Laureano Gómez, publisher of *El Siglo*, a paper of nationwide influence which ranted against Russia, the United States, the United Nations, labor, irreligiosity, Protestantism, Freemasonry, and most other contemporary views as well as different schools of thought. The other was Alberto Lleras Camargo. He has become since 1945 the best known and most important political leader of contemporary Colombia. He had begun his career with the left-wing López Liberals, but later associated himself with the moderate Santos wing, and after that found his own way to the top. When López resigned and left office in 1945, Lleras Camargo became provisional president of Colombia. Colombian conservatives were drawn more than ever toward the disciplined orderliness to be found in the Catholic religion and contemporary authoritarian governments. Many Conservatives quietly rested content with the defection of right-wing Liberals into a coalition of Conservatives and Liberals. This grouping of the Right, later to be known as the National Union, revived both the name and the coalition forged by Dr. Rafael Núñez late in the nineteenth century when he signed the Concordat with the Vatican. While temporary president Lleras effected the revivification of the National Union. Combining the right-wing and moderate Liberals with the left-wing and moderate Conservatives, was the new National Union of 1945 the forerunner of the National Front coalition which, since 1957, has managed the political rule of the country.

The internal political hostility against President López after 1942 was, if anything, even more acute than the social and economic criticism during his first term. His office coincided with those World War II years that were the darkest for the Allies. Colombian politics crackled with Falangist, Nazi, Fascist, and Hispanidad sympathies. Even the Japanese were defended. Gómez' *El Siglo* no less than the influential Jesuit magazine *Revista Xaveriana* attacked López' policy of cooperation with the United States. Class, nationalist, and authoritarian sympathies were challenged by the 400,000 members of the Colombian Federation of Labor. Although López inherited his foreign policy from Santos, who broke relations with Japan, Germany, and Italy in 1942, López went further, declaring war on Germany in 1943. He was the first to give international scope to Colombian Liberalism, which would later put Colombian troops into Korea and Israel for the United Nations.

The internal political situation became so tense that in 1943 López left for the United States on a leave of absence from his presidency. The Conservative-Liberal bloc stopped his legislative program. On his return, Colombian labor unions and thousands of his followers gave him an extraordinary public demonstration. The Colombian Senate rejected his offer to resign. The Conservatives, under the aegis of Laureano Gómez' *El Siglo*, launched a virulent attack. Gómez was arrested. Conservative and nationalist demonstrations followed, devolving into street fighting. A military uprising broke out in July 1944 in the southern, traditionally Conservative, regions. Some officers, emulating the contemporary Argentine example of intervention, tried to overthrow the government. They seized López and some members of his cabinet, but their revolt failed for lack of organization, time, and effort.

Late in 1944 Laureano Gómez was expelled into exile. But the Conservatives were to have their moment. A few months later, in 1945, López resigned the presidency. After fifteen years out of high office, Colombian Conservatism—now mingled more closely than ever before with militarism, *Hispanidad,* and Catholicism—renewed its drive to capture high office. At this time, in 1945, Alberto Lleras Camargo appealed for a Liberal-Conservative combine to govern the country. The Colombian Congress then called upon Lleras Camargo to assume the presidency until the elections of 1946.

Lleras Camargo as President

As Lleras Camargo took the presidency in 1945, he seemed a leader of great ability, promise, and leadership. Countering the popular front programs of the left and center parties, he advanced a program calling for unity and slow growth. Illiteracy is ever the enemy of change. The hindrance of widespread illiteracy to a government which increasingly sought to influence and control popular opinion became all the more glaring. Most of the lower classes, especially those isolated on farms and in the villages and towns, retained the Conservative outlook. It proved difficult to overcome the fixed habits of large masses of people who had long looked to the rich elite and to the Church for advice and opinion.

Lleras Camargo dealt in the coin of popular Liberalism. He wielded the charm of the Liberal label, but in practice he reached out only for Conservatives and moderate Liberals to bring into his cabinet. Some of the economic programs set up between 1932 and 1942 had come to stay; the Lleras Camargo coalition government, like the moderate Santos government earlier, would build upon them. Government and business interest in a nationally developed iron and steel plant increased, and Lleras Camargo preserved the 1938 law which allowed the government to buy and own 51 per cent of the iron and steel company stock. As one of the measures intended to bring about changes in the way of life of the lower classes, the government passed in 1948 a "prohibition law," which outlawed the sale of *chicha* (corn whisky) but encouraged the sale of beer.

In trade union matters, the Lleras Camargo government restrained and limited labor's political activity, seeking to prevent the development of a labor party by channeling labor support into the existing parties. In an action by which the administration forcibly ended the strike of Magdalena River workers, the government made it clear that it would regulate Colombian trade unions so as to allow autonomy under government supervision. By making use of the paternalistic government power which López' laws had instituted, the Lleras Camargo government was able to reduce labor's political pressure. He confined the expenditure of trade union funds and union activities to purely union matters. A law of 1946 prohibited trade unions from assuming a political or religious character. In view of the limited size of the Catholic trade unions and the rising political consciousness of the labor federation unions, the law would seem a hindrance to the natural (but to the government, unnatural) preference of unions for López' kind of political action, or even for the small amount of Communism in Colombia. The 1946 law brought results. The Colombian Federation of Labor entered a period of decline; the Medellín Labor Congress of 1946 revealed internal disunities. Colombian labor did not view Lleras Camargo as a friend, but as one of his last acts, just before the elections of 1946, the government stipulated that all persons holding office in the unions must be workers—a qualification which was a blow against both Communist organizers and intellectuals.

Lleras Camargo also had a strong international sense combined with his sense of conciliation and national unity. In 1946 he appointed ex-President López to the Colombian delegation to the newly created United Nations. Within the Inter-American scene, Lleras Camargo represented Colombia at the Chapultepec (Mexico City) and San Francisco conferences of 1945. When his term of office expired in 1946 he became the first Latin American to be director-general of the Pan-American Union. He was instrumental in bringing to Bogotá in 1948 the historic meeting of the Inter-American states out of which came the Charter of the OAS. He has served as rector of the famous University of the Andes. Under the rotation of office arrangement which followed the reconstructed National Union of 1957, Alberto Lleras Camargo was president of Colombia for a full term (1958-62). He became a member of the Advisory Council of the Alliance for Progress (1963).

Following the elections of 1946, Mariano Ospina Pérez became the first Conservative, noncoalition president since 1930. The Ospina clan, we have seen, was one of the most influential political families in the country. The Liberal disunity still prevailed in 1946. The Santos moderate wing had left the National Union bloc to nominate Gabriel Turbay, a moderate Liberal. Labor and the López wing supported Jorge Eliecer Gaitán. Ospina drew the backing of those who feared radicalism, those who supported national unity, and those who read and believed the editorial alarm voiced in Laureano Gómez' *El Siglo*. Ospina won. A minority president, his 523,000 votes were 200,000 less than the combined Liberal vote. Turbay obtained 401,000 votes to 332,000 for Gaitán, which indicated what a basically large support the Liberals could offer in unity, and proved the mass appeal of Gaitán. A small part of Gaitán's vote came from the small Communist Party, particularly from Bogotá.

Gaitán is a name that still evokes strong argument in Colombia today. A left-of-center Liberal, whom some have called radical, even Communist, he was a leader who fulminated "against the exploitation of the Colombian masses by an alliance between the oligarchies of both parties." [3] For years he agitated and aroused public debate over working-class causes and social reform legislation. He became famous by his defense of the Colombian workers during the 1928 strike against the United Fruit Company. He grew so prominent as to be frightening to Conservatives from 1942 to 1948. He had great oratorical and demogogic appeal for the masses. Ambitious, able, popular as much because of his promises as for his speaking ability, Gaitán was the major postwar figure of the left. It was hard for some people to tell whether he was inspired by his own oratory to make promises merely as any demogogue would, or whether he was a sincere democratic reformer who was interested in getting a new deal for the Colombian masses. He was in some respects a forerunner of Fidel Castro, who had met Gaitán in Bogotá in 1948. Some saw in Gaitán, an admirer of Mussolini, a potential counterpart of Juan Perón of Argentina. His followers were swept along with enthusiasm for advanced social and labor party platforms. Another honest critic found Gaitán to be be a "demagogue" who "talked like Hitler," a political leader of loose promises or a vociferous enemy of the wealthy oligarchy. Whatever he was, Gaitán could have been far more important on the political stage than his 340,000 votes in 1946 indicated. His public image today is still one of a man of the hour, a tribune of the people, and the voice of doom for the "reactionaries."

The Bogotazo

On April 9, 1948, an assassin killed Jorge Gaitán in the streets of Bogotá. It was less than two years after Ospina's inauguration, at a time when a full meeting of the future OAS was taking place in the city. The Secretary of State of the United States, General George C. Marshall, was in Bogotá. The killing of Gaitán and the violent aftermath is still called the bogotazo. Before Gaitán's death in 1948, inflation and labor difficulties had kept radical political discussion and labor demands at a high pitch. Gaitán's admitted power to win votes, his grasp of economic and social forces, made him more prominent than ever. Individuals in both wings of the Liberal Party were already approaching him to talk about candidacy for president in the elections of 1950. Gaitán was strong enough to endanger the

National Union idea. His presence would leave the Conservatives exposed as a minority, if he should lead the Liberals. His pressure induced Liberals to leave the Ospina cabinet; he influenced Liberals in congress as well as the trade unions. He preached return to independent Liberal politics and political victory.[4]

Conservatives and Liberals: IV

In the fifteen years following the rioting and destruction which took place in Bogotá—indeed throughout the country—after Gaitán's death, an estimated 200,000 people had lost their lives in the disorders that followed. The elimination of Gaitán and the grave threat of civil war (charged to the Communists) induced a resumption of the coalition tendency in the government. Leading Liberals again came to the aid of the Conservative administration in the interests of order and national security. But in spite of the unity arranged at the top by political and business leaders, there remained bitter hatreds among rank-and-file Liberals and Conservatives.

The unsettled religious, class and socioeconomic antagonisms rose to the point where the Conservatives were accused of failing to maintain the stability and respect for law and order which they respected so much. After the first years of this tension, the Liberals again left the cabinet. This gave them independent political action, but did not restore internal peace. By 1949 it seemed that there was little hope of restoring the National Union. The domestic situation was not soothed when President Ospina broke diplomatic relations with Soviet Russia in 1949. It was perhaps better for peace and quiet that the government had prohibited the sale of *chicha*.

The Conservatives won the post-Gaitán elections of 1950. Liberals offered no candidate and boycotted the elections. The Conservative candidate, and successful president, was Laureano Gómez. As an ultraconservative, newspaper publisher, and a senator, Laureano Gómez had amply revealed his pro-German, neofascist, anti-American, and antidemocratic sentiments. The national government was now under the leadership of a man who was fully at home in the authoritarian doctrines and disciplines of the twentieth-century fascist state.

[4] Vernon Fluharty, *Dance of the Millions: Military Rule and the Social Revolution in Colombia*, 1930-56 (Pittsburgh, 1957), pp. 70-71, 201-203.

Gómez took over a Colombia which had a population of 10 million in an area approximately half the size of Argentina, but larger than Texas, California, and Massachusetts combined, the fourth largest Latin American country in point of population.

Gómez was a Conservative nationalist. Like Santos, Ospina, and Lleras Camargo, Laureano Gómez as President was of no mind to turn the clock back on the business, social, and industrial gains which had taken root. The control and regulation of labor was, as expected, more severe and tight than Liberals would have allowed, but none of the basic social and welfare laws were repealed. They may not have been fully enforced, but at least they were not rescinded. The Gómez administration, like other Conservatives in business and in other sections of the country, kept up the drive for industrialization. National industry was pushed; the steel plant was still viewed as the great symbol of national growth. Turned down by North American finance, Gómez turned to European capital for the funds necessary to open the Paz del Rio steel plant. Gómez was determined to have a steel plant—fifteen years of planning and favorable legislation could not be set aside. It has since come into active production.

Gómez submitted very large budgets in 1951 and 1952, in which the large public works appropriation came first and army requests second. Public education, health and welfare came a good deal behind. Colombia's needs for roads, bridges, and internal improvements —especially railways—had always been of major importance. All recent Colombian governments have increased the pace of communications, railroad, and airport construction. The Atlantic Railway, connecting the Caribbean with the Central Magdalena Valley and Bogotá, had high significance. That road was not opened until 1961; in 1963 it received modern diesel locomotives to haul its freight cars.

It was equally important to connect Bogotá with Medellín and Cali. The extension of coffee planting, exports and trade down toward Cali and Buenaventura had strong political effects. The growth of commerce and business had made the business classes of Cali and their dependent workmen supporters of the Liberals, for the most part. In a parallel way, great profits from oil exports had enriched government coffers and private business in the northern region along the Caribbean. Government public works were extended to help Cartagena and Barranquilla, on the Pacific coast. We have already

seen in Chapter One the picture of the cultural growth of Cali, especially the University of Cali, whose medical school and library are
aided by the Rockefeller Foundation.

Gómez inherited for more than a decade the bitter legacy of civil
war, banditry, Liberal attacks on the Conservatives, and Conservative
attacks on the Liberals. He had little opportunity to turn his attention to basic matters, because he had only a year in which to govern. Although he softened his pro-Hitlerism and did not practice what
he had preached editorially, revolt broke out against him. Gómez
went into exile in Franco's Spain. Sick and aging, he showed more
strength against this opposition than he had shown in office, but his
attempt to hold his power and maintain public order with a "state of
siege" were a failure.

The Military

The civil war spread. In June 1953 some Liberals and some Conservatives accepted the plot of some generals to depose Gómez. The
way was now open for Colombia to fall into military dictatorship.
Gustavo Rojas Pinilla, former Colonel, seized the government at the
head of a military junta. But Rojas Pinilla, who never was modest in
his view of his role, did not feel any sense of obligation to the civilians
who had helped him come in.

Rojas Pinilla, president from 1953 to 1957, has been described as
one of the most "savage, venal and altogether incompetent administrators in the history of the nation." [5] The military era of the past
decade closed its first upon Colombian intellectual life as well as
politics. Like his Venezuelan counterpart and contemporary, Marcos
Pérez Jiménez, he ruled Colombia by force and decrees, and did not
neglect to enrich himself in the process. He closed down the press;
even *El Tiempo* was suspended.

The Civilian and the Coalition

Rojas Pinilla did one good thing in politics: he forced Liberals and
Conservatives to come together to get rid of him. As we have seen,
Alberto Lleras Camargo, who went all the way to Spain to get Gómez'
agreement, negotiated the pact between Liberals and Conservatives

[5] Hubert Herring, *History of Latin America,* 2nd ed. (New York, 1961), pp.
519-20.

that revived the National Union. The Church approved, and so did other generals hostile to Rojas Pinilla. The new constitution convention of 1957, which Rojas Pinilla had himself called to placate national opinion and which he had prepared to control, opened the way to a new era without him.

Rojas Pinilla thought of his regime as linking politics with business. An "industrial revolution" would put people to work and stimulate the business classes. The fact was that his administration coincided with expanding production and prosperity. It also coincided with great speculation and a wave of inflation which undermined the very values which had been built up. The Rojas Pinilla expansion led directly to the very austerity which had to replace it later on. Similarly, the excessive power of his dictatorship generated the opposition which led to his fall. For all the money he made for himself and for a new rich class, it was still possible to organize a general strike which led to his overthrow. Furthermore, a popular plebiscite endorsed the political pact to replace him.

The new day of the coalition forged by Lleras Camargo opened with unusual provisions. The pledge of women's suffrage satisfied Liberals, while the guarantee of the continued establishment of Catholicism pleased the Conservatives. Both parties must have hoped for much from the understanding that school and education were to get 10 per cent of the national budget. Certainly schools were left far behind by the Rojas Pinilla administration, compared to the materialistic emphasis in development. The contemporary scene, as indicated in Chapter One, is so far one of domestic peace and material progress under this unique political arrangement.

SUGGESTED READINGS

Reading resources on the national period of northern South America are found in the same hard way as natural resources: by persistent digging. It is surprising how little has appeared in recent times on the countries with which we are concerned. There is even less on the Bolivarian and Gran Colombian aspects of the early internationalism in their history. Moreover, the balance of literature is uneven: more exists on Colombia than on Venezuela. Panama is without any adequate bookshelf; on the other hand, British Guiana has some sound studies.

The history of the region, more than its culture, contains two of the greatest names on the South American continent or on the shores of the Caribbean: Bolívar and Miranda. Travel literature, epics of navigation and exploration, tales of the marauders of the age of buccaneers, the bold strikes of the Spanish Conquest—these still win literary attention. It is strange, however, that the area and its heroes have not attracted European or Hollywood film leaders to set a vivid picture before the public. Certainly the epic, the romance and clash, the drama of men and events, great battles, the extraordinary natural scenery, the beauty and influence of women, are the stuff of a fine audio-visual aid. Most literature, however, remains in the social sciences, while art and cultural expression are not in the forefront.

The literature has to be dug out from general and textbook accounts on over-all Latin American history, geography, and economics, rather than in useful national single-country studies of Colombia and Venezuela. One of the best of these texts is John E. Fagg, *Latin America: A General History* (New York, 1963), with chapters on Venezuela and Colombia. Harry Bernstein, *Modern and Contemporary Latin America*

(Chicago, 1952), has a consecutive narrative of modern Colombia (100 pages; Chaps. 32-36).

Most historical, social, cultural, and economic materials and books are in Spanish, although some good titles can be found in English. The *Travels* of the noted Prussian savant, Alexander von Humboldt, are a mine of information and present a valuable point of view. During our own era, biographies in English for Francisco de Miranda and Simón Bolívar have been published. Popular and travel books on both Colombia and Venezuela, some of which are very well written, may be satisfying to many readers. Ethnological work in English has been authoritatively laid down for both Andean and circum-Caribbean Indians in the indispensable *Handbook of South American Indians* published by the Smithsonian Institution. A great scarcity of material exists in political science and in social-community studies. Colombian sociology and regional studies have produced some four or five community studies of village, town, and subregions.

Monthly magazines, notably *Américas* (trilingual) and *Current History*, frequently publish cultural and historical articles on our "Bolivarian" countries, while the weeklies *Time* and *Newsweek* devote news-pages to items of current significance. *The New York Times* has scattered and irregular reports. For a large yearly listing of articles, essays and books see the relevant headings for Venezuela and Colombia in the annual *Handbook of Latin American Studies*. Basic historical articles appear frequently in the *Hispanic American Historical Review*. The *Hispanic Report* is valuable. See also the annual series on the Caribbean, published by the University of Florida Press. The 1962 Caribbean conference of the University of Florida dealt with Colombia.

From Panama to British Guiana is a vast journey, and reading guides are harder to find than for Colombia and Venezuela. One basic study is Raymond T. Smith's *The Negro Family in British Guiana* (London, 1956). The "left-wing" Guianese leader Cheddi Jagan wrote *Forbidden Freedom: The Story of British Guiana* (London, 1954). The problems of the Guianan Negro and family, or of society and politics—especially on the current scene—have stimulated more accounts than has Panama. Writings in English begin with Sir Walter Raleigh, and British scholarship, and the acute social investigators of the University College of the West Indies (in Jamaica) have contributed a good deal to Guianese sociological study. Currently, the radicalism of Cheddi Jagan, Negro-East Indian-white attitudes, and the fate of federation, colonialism, or self-government have earned some attention in North American newspapers and journals.

Books on Colombia which deal with the events of the present generation (since 1932) include W. O. Galbraith, *Colombia: A General Survey* (London, 1953); John Hunter, *Emerging Colombia* (Washington, D.C., 1962); Vernon Fluharty, *Dance of the Millions: Military Rule and Social*

Revolution in Colombia, 1930-56 (Pittsburgh, 1957); and John D. Martz, *Colombia: A Contemporary Political Survey* (Chapel Hill, 1962). Current affairs predominate in these titles. The chief work on history, not too estimable but still used in Colombian secondary schools, is J. M. Henao and G. Arrubla, *History of Colombia*, translated by J. Fred Rippy (Chapel Hill, 1938). A more popular work of a few years ago is Kathleen Romoli's *Colombia: Gateway to South America* (New York, 1941). David Bushnell has written a good history of *The Santander Regime in Gran Colombia* (Newark, Delaware, 1954).

Most of the sociological, community, and cultural geographic studies on Colombia are quite good. Their titles describe the subject. Alphabetically, they are Raymond E. Crist, *The Cauca Valley, Colombia: Land Tenure and Land Use* (Baltimore, 1952); Orlando Fals-Borda, *Peasant Society in the Colombian Andes: A Sociological Study of Saucío* (Gainesville, 1935), by an able Colombian sociologist trained in the United States; James J. Parsons, *Antioqueño Colonization in Western Colombia* (Berkeley, 1949), an outstanding cultural history as well as a geography; Gerardo and Alicia Reichel-Dolmatoff, *The People of Aritama. The Cultural Personality of a Colombian Mestizo Village* (Chicago, 1961), a detailed community study of society, people, and psychology; T. Lynn Smith, *Tabio: A Study of Rural Organization* (Washington. D.C., 1945), an early study for the Department of Agriculture by a noted Latin Americanist sociologist of the University of Florida; and Robert C. West, *The Pacific Lowlands of Colombia* (Baton Rouge, 1957), an original description by an able geographer.

Venezuela offers two studies of the dictator-type in Thomas Rourke, *Gómez, Tyrant of the Andes* (New York, 1936), and George S. Wise, *Caudillo: A Portrait of Antonio Guzmán Blanco* (New York, 1951). On a major institution of Venezuelan economic history see Roland D. Hussey, *The Caracas Company, 1728-1784* (Cambridge, Mass., 1943). A useful and general history is William D. and Amy Marsland, *Venezuela through its History* (New York, 1954). For the issue of Church and State in Venezuelan history, see Mary Watters, *A History of the Church in Venezuela, 1810-1930* (Chapel Hill, 1933).

Among the few books on current affairs in Venezuela, essentially background, are Arthur P. Whitaker, *The United States and South America: the Northern Republics* (Cambridge, Mass., 1948). More specific is Edwin Lieuwen, *Venezuela* (New York, 1961) and his earlier *Petroleum in Venezuela: A History* (Berkeley, 1954). In his *Acción Democrática of Venezuela: its Origin and Development*, Latin American Monographs, 9 (Gainesville, 1959), Stanley J. Serxner has made available an admiring, yet useful, slender outline of the rise of Rómulo Betancourt and his political program in the current Venezuelan scene.

Although Venezuela and Colombia have distinguished historians, national academies of history, and journals of history, most historical writings and publications deal with their colonial history and independence. National, economic, and intellectual history characterizes foreign historical writing on these two countries. The personalist traditions in politics and the strong role of the individual in their culture has influenced a large amount of biographical writing. Here, too, the remote past and national origins receive far more attention than the recent past and present. Most biographies deal over and over again with the same founding fathers: Bolívar, Miranda, Santander, Páez, Torres, Nariño, and lesser lights of that day.

INDEX

Venezuela

COLOMBIA